CENTRAL WALES

160 pages o

CW00661144

BEST IN CENTRAL WALES

Editor: Anwen Sian Parry

including
Cader Idris and Dyfi valley
Northern Ceredigion
Montgomeryshire and
Radnorshire

First published in 2015
© original authors/Carreg Gwalch
© Carreg Gwalch 2015

ISBN: 978-1-84524-219-0

Published by Gwasg Carreg Gwalch,
12 Iard yr Orsaf, Llanrwst, Wales
LL26 0EH   tel: 01492 642031
email: books@carreg-gwalch.com
website: www.carreg-gwalch.com

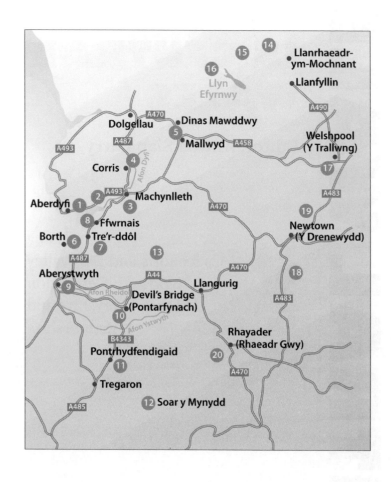

Contents

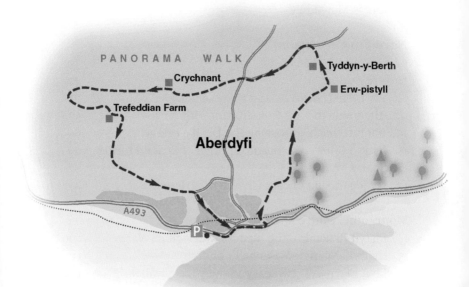

Walk 1
Aberdyfi – Erw-pistyll – Trefeddian Farm – Aberdyfi

Walk details

Approx distance: *4 miles/6.5 kilometres*

Approx time: *About 2½ hours*

O.S. Maps: *1:50 000 Landranger Sheet 135*
1:25 000 Explorer OL 23

Start: *The car park on the sea front in Aberdyfi.*
Grid Ref. SN 612 959

Access: *Aberdyfi is on the A493, south of Tywyn, and 10*
miles west of Machynlleth. Trains on the Cambrian
Coast Line stop here. Bus 29 from Machynlleth or
Tywyn.

Parking: *On the sea front, behind the beach, in Aberdyfi.*

Going: *Moderate – paths, tracks and lanes.*

Points of Interest:

[1] **Aberdyfi,** translated into English, means 'the mouth of the Dyfi'. Backed by steep hills to the north, this picturesque resort is situated where the river flows into Cardigan Bay. The name of the village became famous in 1785 when Charles Dibdin composed the song 'The Bells of Aberdyfi'. A comic

Welsh character sang the lyrics in the Drury Lane musical 'Liberty Hall'. There are several stories about the bells. One tells of a giant who sat on Cadair Idris and lost his bell, which he had used as a paddle on Afon Dyfi during a storm. Another tells of bells around the necks of lost sheep, as in southern Europe.

[2] The best known story is that of **'Cantre'r Gwaelod'**, the story of the submerging of lands in Cardigan Bay. Although the inundation probably took place at the end of the last Ice Age, the legend places the event in the 6th century when, it is said, the plain had several churches with beautiful chimes. According to the legend, because of the negligence of the drunken dyke keeper Seithennyn, a great storm breached the walls, and the plain, its towns and inhabitants were lost forever. Some people say that on windless nights, distant chimes may be heard, rising from the sea bed. The old boundaries of Cantre'r Gwaelod are believed to exist in the form of submerged reefs with Sarn y Bwch to the north (near Tywyn) and Sarn Cynfelyn

(between Borth and Aberystwyth) to the south.

[3] Little is known of Aberdyfi until 1216, when Llywelyn ap Iorwerth summoned all

Welsh rulers to meet him at Aberdyfi. Although popular with herring fishermen, records show Aberdyfi had only three houses in 1569. Less than thirty years later, in 1597, the **Bear of Amsterdam** and its crew of sixty-five Spanish sailors drifted into the Dyfi estuary. Westerly winds prevented her from sailing out, and the Welsh militia did not have the means to take or destroy the ship. It is said that some Spaniards swam ashore and, after hiding in the hills, merged with the local families. When the wind eventually changed, the *Bear of Amsterdam* sailed away but was captured by Drake's navy. In remembrance of this event, there is a café in Aberdyfi called the 'Bear of Amsterdam'.

[4] Aberdyfi grew into a busy port and wool, timber and oak bark were exported in the 18th century. Ships were built here and Aberdyfi became the **port for the Dyfi valley** with the development of local lead, copper and slate mines. A jetty over 100 metres long permitted ships to be unloaded and loaded at all states of the tide. Nowadays, Aberdyfi is well known for its sailing and water sports.

[5] On a clear day there are superb views from this lane and other points on the route, of the **Dyfi estuary**, Ynys-las, Borth

7

and around the Cardigan Coast to the cliffs of Penfro (Pembrokeshire).

Walk Directions:
[-] denotes Point of Interest

1. From the car park on the sea front in Aberdyfi [1], turn right and pass the Tourist Information Centre and gardens on your right. Pass the church on your left and in approximately 100 metres you will reach the Literary Institute. Cross the road to take a path that rises above the road. It zigzags to some steps and eventually emerges on a road.

2. Turn right a few paces then bear left up steps. Go right then bear left and then right again to reach a narrow path that goes uphill through gorse. The path is part of the Welsh Coastal Path. Cross a stile and walk uphill passing a small stable on your right and bearing slightly left to a yellow post.

3. Continue ahead on the path. There are fine views of the Dyfi estuary on your right. Pass a waymarked post and bear left along the hill slope to pass above a valley.

4. Go through a small wooden gate. Farther along, go through another gate and walk uphill to a stile. In another 50 metres cross the stream on your right and climb a ladder stile.

5. Walk up the field and in approximately 80 metres bear left through a gap into another field. Bear right and continue uphill. Go through a gap in the bushes into the next field and walk towards the left side of farm buildings. Turn left to a gate then go through another gate onto a track coming from the farm, Erw-Pistyll.

6. Turn left to go through a gate across the track. Walk uphill to reach a lane where there are some fine views of the Dyfi Estuary and Ynys Las. The lane you will join is aptly named "Panorama Walk" [5]. Turn left downhill and cross a cattle grid. The track now goes through farmland. On reaching a junction with another lane, cross directly to a track.

Trefeddian Fach farm ruins

7. Continue ahead to a farm. The lane bends right to a farmhouse. Do not go as far as the farmhouse but go

through the left gate on your left. Walk diagonally to the top right corner of the field to a wooden gate. Continue walking beside the fence on your right.

8. When you reach a surfaced track, turn left downhill. There are beautiful views of Bae Ceredigion from this point. Walk around a small hill and descend to a grassy track to reach two ruined farm buildings.

9. Pass the ruined farm buildings on your left and walk around the hillside. Descend to a stile below a farm. Cross a plank over a stream and walk uphill to a footpath sign on the left. Bear left and go through another gate into a field. Bear right to pass the farmhouse on your right.

10. Follow a fence on your right to a fenced corner. Turn right to cross a stream and shortly follow a fence on your right. The path rises gently. Walk over the hill, under the wooden masts to a wooden bench. From here there are fine views of the coast and the Dyfi estuary.

11. Climb over a stile at a fenced corner then follow the fence on your right to another stile. Pass behind

bungalows and cross a ladder stile.

12. Cross directly over a road to the road directly opposite. Follow this road until it ends, then continue on a track. When the

Aberdyfi

track ends at a gate, go ahead on a path on your left between two hedges and metal railings.

St Peter's Church and Terrace Road

13. On reaching a junction, turn left to emerge on a road. Turn right and pass under the railway bridge. At a junction, walk ahead to reach the A493 in Aberdyfi. Turn right to the start of the walk and car park.

Facilities:
Pubs and cafes in Aberdyfi. Public toilets near the start. Visitor Centre.

Originally published in
Circular Walks in the Dyfi Valley

by Dorothy Hamilton

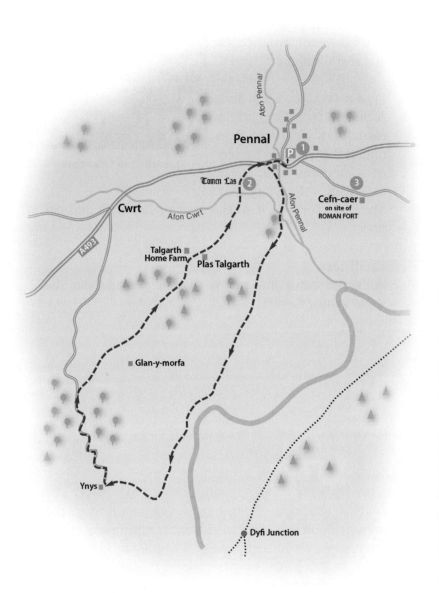

Walk 2
Pennal – Afon Dyfi – Plas Talgarth – Pennal

Walk details

Approx distance: *3½ miles/5.8 kilometres*

Approx time: *2 hours*

O.S. Maps: *1:50 000 Landranger Sheet 135*
                 1:25 000 Explorer OL 23

Start: *Pennal Church. Grid Ref. SH 699 003*

Access: *Pennal is on the A493, west of Machynlleth. Buses*
                 from Machynlleth and Tywyn.

Parking: *Behind the church by the public toilets.*

Going: *Easy – field, riverside and woodland paths, lanes.*

Points of Interest:

[1] **Pennal church** is the only one in Wales to be dedicated to St Peter ad Vincula (St Peter in Chains). St Tannwg and St Eithrias, Celtic missionaries from Brittany, founded a church here in the sixth century, but it was rededicated by the Normans five hundred years later. It has been rebuilt several times since. The circular churchyard indicates early origins. Although the present church is mainly Victorian, it contains some interesting features, including a 'Green Man' in the East Window. Look for the facsimile of the Pennal Letter sent by Owain Glyndŵr in 1406 to the French King Charles VI. In the letter he pledged allegiance to the French Pope in Avignon – at that time Europe had two

*Owain Glyndŵr memorial
at Pennal church*

Popes – provided certain conditions were met. Although normally kept in Paris archives, the original letter was loaned to the National Library at Aberystwyth for six months in AD 2000 as part of an exhibition about Owain Glyndŵr's life. Pennal church was Owain Glyndŵr's Chapel Royal in the year 1406 and he may have signed the letter here.

[2] The tree covered mound, **Tomen Las,** is thought to be the site of the medieval court from where Owain Glyndŵr sent the 'Pennal Letter' in 1406.

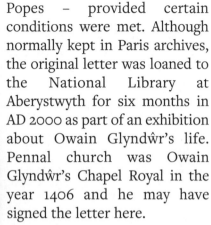

[3] **Cefn Caer farm** is built in the west corner of the Roman fort. In the field, to the east of the farm, there are signs of foundations in the form of grassy embankments. The fort was sited on Sarn Helen, the Roman road from Caerhun (near Conwy) to *Moridunum* at Caerfyrddin. Roman coins and pottery have been found on the site.

Cefn Caer farmhouse

Walk Directions: **[–] denotes Point of Interest**
1.   Face Pennal church [1] and turn left along the A493 to cross the bridge over Afon Pennal. In about 40 metres turn left through a broad gate onto a track.

2.   Continue ahead to walk beside the river. Go through a gate across the track. At this point, the track bears right, away from the river. Cross a bridge over a stream and immediately bear right to go through a field gate.

3.   Slant left to reach a stream and continue through the field with the ditch on your right. Pass alongside woodland. When you reach the end of the field go through a small gate and cross a ladder stile.

4.   Walk on beside the stream until you reach a footbridge across it. Cross and turn left. In a few metres, veer slightly right to follow another ditch on your right.

5.   On reaching the end of the field, cross a boggy ditch then climb to the top of an embankment and turn right to cross a stile. Afon Dyfi is now on your left. Walk along the embankment and ignore a stile below on the right.

6.   Look for a footbridge on the right and, after crossing it, walk ahead with a ditch on the left. Before

reaching the end of the field, go through a gate on your left. Walk along the fence on your right to a gate straight ahead. Turn left and walk towards the farmhouse. Go through a gate to the right of it.

7.   Walk up to the lane and follow it uphill. Ignore a track on the left. Continue along the undulating lane. Pass some houses, a track to Penmaenbach, and a bungalow on the left.

8.   When the lane descends, cross a stile near a gate on the right. Walk up the field and, at the top of a knoll, go through a gate. Bear slightly left, then right, to pass between buildings.

9.   Walk ahead and go through a gate into a field. Continue ahead uphill towards woodland – from here there are fine views of the estuary.

10.   On reaching a fence, go through a kissing gate into a strip of woodland. A clear path goes slightly downhill and, in a few metres, has a fence on the right.

11.   Follow the path as it levels then goes slightly uphill to a stile. Continue beside the fence and cross a stile into a wood. In a few metres, ignore a path on the left, and walk ahead.

On joining a wider path, turn left.

Plas Talgarth

12. The path emerges at the Plas Talgarth holiday complex. Walk ahead to reach the access drive and continue along it to a junction. Turn left to follow a lane between fields which leads to the A493.

13. After crossing a stream, you will see the mound, Tomen Las [2] on your right. On reaching the A493, turn right to return to the church in Pennal.

14. If you have time to spare, and would like to see the site of the Roman fort at Pennal, continue along the A493 for about 100 metres, then turn right along a lane. Follow it for about 600 metres, to just beyond the farm of Cefn Caer [3].

Facilities:
Refreshments at the Riverside Hotel. Public toilets behind the church.

Originally published in
Circular Walks in the Dyfi Valley

by Dorothy Hamilton

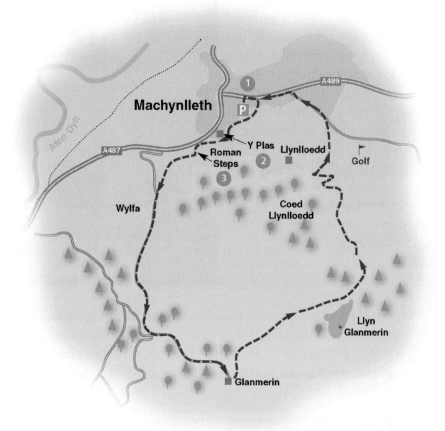

Walk 3

Machynlleth – Roman Steps – Llyn Glanmerin – Machynlleth

Walk details

Approx distance: *4 miles/6.5 kilometres*

Approx time: *About 2½ hours*

O.S. Maps: *1:50 000 Landranger Sheet 135*
1:25 000 Explorer OL 23

Start: *Car park off Maengwyn Street in Machynlleth. Grid Ref. SH 747 007.*

Access: *Machynlleth is on the A489, between Dolgellau and Aberystwyth. Trains from Shrewsbury, Aberystwyth and Pwllheli. Buses from Newtown, Dolgellau, Tywyn and Aberystwyth.*

Parking: *Town car park off Maengwyn Street, between Machynlleth Library and the antique shop.*

Going: *Moderate – field and moorland paths, lanes.*

Points of Interest:

[1] Visit **Machynlleth** on a Wednesday, when Heol Maengwyn is lined with colourful market stalls. In 1291, Edward I granted the Lord of Powys a charter to hold a market at Machynlleth every Wednesday for ever, and two fairs a year. Machynlleth was the town chosen by Owain Glyndŵr to be the capital of Wales. In 1404 it is thought he was crowned here before envoys from Scotland, France and Castile. He held Parliament on the site of Parliament House. North of the clock tower stands Royal House. According to local tradition it is

Y Plas, Machynlleth

the building where Dafydd Gam was imprisoned after trying to assassinate Owain Glyndŵr, whilst he was being crowned. Henry Tudor is said to have stayed here on his way to Bosworth Field. King Charles may have visited in 1644. An underground passage is said to run from the house to and under Afon Dyfi, as far as Pennal. The impressive 78 foot (24m) high clock tower was built in 1874 to celebrate the 21st birthday of Viscount Castlereagh, eldest son of the 5th Marquess of Londonderry.

[2] In the early part of the 19th century, **Y Plas** was owned by Sir John Edwards, and it passed to the Londonderry family through marriage. The mansion is mainly 17th century, with 19th century additions. Famous people who have visited Y Plas include Edward VII and Queen Alexandra. It was given to the town in the 1930s and was home to *Celtica*, a Celtic heritage centre. Today, Y Plas facilitates a restaurant and an art gallery.

[3] **Roman Steps** The steps were probably cut several centuries later than the Roman period. The Romans probably came this way, however, on their way to the small fort on the hill called Wylfa. It would have been

a lookout post for the larger fort at Pennal.

Walk Directions:
[–] denotes Point of Interest
1.   From the car park in Machynlleth [1], walk out to Heol Maengwyn (the A489) and turn right. Pass the library on your right and, in another 20 metres, bear right through gates to follow a track.

2.   The track veers to the right alongside a football ground. Pass the Leisure Centre on your right and shortly turn left to pass Y Plas [2], on your right. Pass a children's playground, and then a field on the left. Follow a path to West Lodge.

3.   After passing the Lodge on your left, immediately bear left on a path to go through a kissing gate with the "Glyndŵr's Way" waymark. It leads to the Roman Steps [3]. Take care when walking up the steps as they can be slippery. Go up the steps and continue on a path. Take a pause and look at the view on your right of Dyffryn Dyfi and Machynlleth where the county of Gwynedd and Powys meet. Go through a kissing gate and cross a track near cottages. Walk uphill on a grassy path to emerge on a lane.

Machynlleth and the Dyfi Hills

4. Turn left along the lane. Ignore a track on the left with the Glyndŵr's Way waymark but follow the Welsh Coastal Path waymark instead. Cross a cattle grid and pass a farm and wood on the right and then a track to a house on the left. Descend the lane and, at the point where it swings right to meet another lane, turn left on a track, to have a stream on your right.

5. Go through the gate for Fferm Glanmerin. Follow the track uphill to the farm. Walk ahead to pass a building on the left. Before reaching the farmhouse, turn left on a track. Follow it to a gate and stream.

6. Walk ahead across the field where there is lovely scenery of Dyffryn Dyfi and the Estuary on your left. In 50 metres, follow a fence on your left and cross a small stream. Continue above the fence and pass some woodland. Ignore a field gate on the left and, in another 50 metres, cross a stile beside a gate.

7. Walk ahead uphill between rocky outcrops. Ignore a gate and fence on the right and bear left. The unclear path shortly bears right to reach a stile at a gate through marshy ground. Pass marshy land on the right and go ahead towards the lake called Llyn Glanmerin. Continue beside it.

8. Walk ahead towards a strip of coniferous forest and cross a stile. Follow a path through the trees to a stile on the other side of the plantation. Go ahead on a

clear path to have the forest on your right.

Llyn Glanmerin

9.   In about 40 metres, you will come across a pole with waymarks. Ignore a gate on the right. Walk ahead but bear slightly left on a clear path to have the forest farther distant on your right.

10. Walk ahead over the common and cross marshy land and boggy pools. Pass a rotten unmarked pole and follow the track downhill. The path veers slightly left towards trees and Machynlleth, which is in view below. Ignore a path on the right going uphill.

11.   Bear left to descend towards trees. Continue beside a wall and trees on the left. Pass above a golf course. The path zigzags –look for posts with yellow arrows – and continue with a fence on the left through boggy land.

12.   After passing a fenced off area, cross a stile and continue ahead to a road. Turn left to a crossroads and turn left along Heol Maengwyn. Pass on your left, a timber framed 17th century house. Continue along the road to the car park and start of the walk.

Facilities:
Public toilets near the start of the walk. Full facilities in Machynlleth. Weekly market on Wednesdays. Owain Glyndŵr Centre. Tourist Information Centre.

Originally published in
Circular Walks in the Dyfi Valley

by Dorothy Hamilton

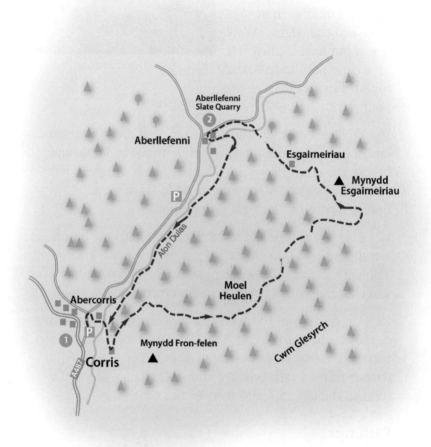

Walk 4
Corris – Moel Heulen – Mynydd Esgairneiriau – Aberllefenni – Afon Dulas – Corris

Walk details

Approx distance: *7 miles/11.5 kilometres*

Approx time: *About 4 hours*

O.S. Maps: *1:50 000 Landranger Sheet 124 or Landranger 135*
                 1:25 000 Explorer OL 23 or Explorer OL 215

Start: *Car park at the Corris Railway Museum.*
                 Grid Ref. SH 754 078

Access: *Corris is off the A487, north of Machynlleth. At the*
                 Braich Goch Hotel, turn right into Corris village.
                 Buses from Dolgellau and Machynlleth.

Parking: *Signposted parking at Corris Railway Museum.*

Going: *Moderate – riverside and forest paths, tracks and*
                 lanes.

Points of Interest:

[1] **Corris** lies in the steep valley of Afon Dulas, surrounded by the remains of slate quarrying. The extraction of slate has been the chief factor in the development of the village, although forestry is now the main industry in the area. The planting of the Dyfi forest began in 1926. The Roman road Sarn Helen passed this way and the Romans may have quarried slate in the area. In 1859, a horse-drawn tramway connected the quarries around Corris with the port at

Derwen-las on the Dyfi. When the Cambrian Railway opened in 1867, the tramway west of Machynlleth became disused. Steam engines were introduced on the Corris Railway line in 1879 and, for a short while, there was a passenger service. The quarries continued to use the line until 1948, when flood damage to the Dyfi Bridge forced its closure. Braich Goch, the largest quarry in Corris, employing about two hundred men, was sited north-east of the village. Since closure in 1971, the area has been landscaped and the main road actually crosses the mill area.

[2] Still in use, the **Aberllefenni quarry** has probably been worked since the 16th century. It produces very high quality slate. The underground workings were connected to the mill by a tramway which was in use until the 1970s. The terminus of the Corris railway was opposite the mill. Remains of the railway can be seen at various places in the valley.

Walk Directions: [–] **denotes Point of Interest**
1.   From the car park walk out to the road and bear right through Corris [1]. After crossing Afon Deri, turn right on a lane downhill. Cross Afon Dulas and follow the lane as it bears right. Continue past houses and walk uphill. Pass a track on the right to Fronfelen Hall.

2.   In about 100 metres, when the lane starts to descend, turn left on a path that rises into the forest. Ignore a signposted track on the left and continue ahead to reach a wider track.

3. Bear left and, on reaching a fork, go right to continue on the wide track. Take care as motocross bikes also use this trail. Walk ahead for 670 metres until you reach a footpath signpost on the right. The trail ascends through forest until you come to a wide track at a crossroad.

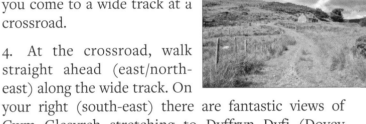

4. At the crossroad, walk straight ahead (east/north-east) along the wide track. On your right (south-east) there are fantastic views of Cwm Glesyrch stretching to Dyffryn Dyfi (Dovey Valley) and beyond. Continue ahead for about 500 metres to a fork and bear left.

5. Keep to the wide track which bends to the right and continues for a kilometre until you reach a gate. Cross this gate and proceed to follow the trail along Mynydd Esgairneiriau. Be wary of any cattle in the fields.  Cross a cattle grid and continue pass a derelict farm building on your right – 'Esgairneiriau'.

6. On this track you can see to the east that on the side of a mountain is a large hole which was the entrance to underground slate workings. The track bends to the left and in about 100 metres leave the trail

by going downhill through the field on your left. Bear right (west) to a wooden gate at the edge of the wood.

7.   Go through the gate and follow the woodland trail downhill. Take care as the path can be slippery due to small streams flowing to Afon Dulas. After walking almost 700 metres the trail bends to the right. At this point there is a small trail on your left leading to a wooden bridge that crosses Nant Esgair-neiriau. Cross the bridge and follow the riverside trail.

8.   In about 300 metres there will be a ruin on your right, turn right to cross a stile and walk downhill along the side of the field. At the bottom, bear left to follow a fence above Afon Dulas. Go through a gate on the right into trees, and walk downhill on a wide track. Emerge in a field and walk ahead.

9.   Climb over a stile near a gate and cross a footbridge over Afon Dulas. Go through some gates and pass a farm building on the left. Follow the farm drive but, before it reaches the lane, bear left to cross an old bridge.

10. Go up some steps to the lane and turn left. Aberllefenni quarries are on the right [2].

11.   Continue along the road and pass the slate mill on the left and houses on the right. Immediately beyond

the road sign for Aberllefenni, turn left downhill into a Forestry picnic site and car park.

12.   When the track turns left, continue on a gravel path to have Afon Dulas on the left.

Aberllefenni Slate Quarry as seen from Esgairneiriau

On reaching a track, turn left to cross a bridge over the river. Immediately turn right on a track.

13. Cross a bridge over a small stream and bear right to a telegraph pole. Walk along a path to pass the garden of the house on the left. Go through a small gate into a field.

14. Walk beside Afon Dulas. Notice the slate in the river. Continue ahead through the fields, crossing stiles. When the last field narrows, walk ahead on a path through woodland, beside the river.

15. Climb over a stile and continue on a clear path some distance from the river. Cross a stream by stepping stones and a fence type stile. Walk through a field by keeping slightly uphill from the river. Pass a small gate on the left and cross a stream. Maintain your direction to reach a broad gate, and enter woodland.

16. Continue ahead on a clear track. Go uphill to join another track. Bear right to pass above a quarry. Go through a broad gate and continue ahead.

17. Emerge on a lane and turn right to retrace your steps into Corris and the start of the walk.

Facilities:
Alternative parking at the Forestry Picnic Site near Aberllefenni. Public toilets near the start. Railway museum. Corris Railway. Cafe at Corris Craft Centre on the A487. King Arthur's Labyrinth. Youth hostel in Corris.

Originally published in
Circular Walks in the Dyfi Valley

by Dorothy Hamilton

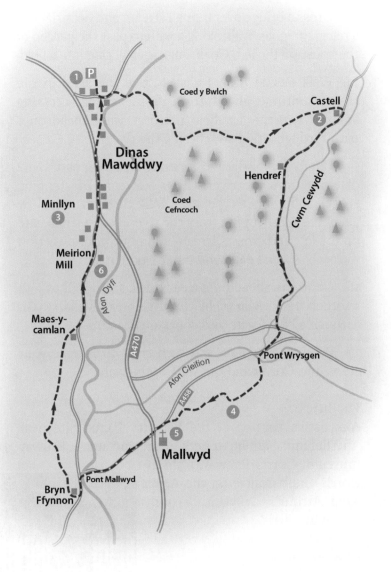

Walk 5

Dinas Mawddwy – Cwm Cewydd –
Mallwyd – Dinas Mawddwy

Walk details

Approx distance: *6½ miles/10.5 kilometres*

Approx time: *About 4 hours*

O.S. Maps: *1:50 000 Landranger Sheet 124*
1:25 000 Explorer OL 23

Start: *Gwesty'r Llew Coch (The Red Lion) in Dinas Mawddwy. Grid Ref. SH 858 148.*

Access: *Dinas Mawddwy is just off the A470, 10 miles (16 km) east of Dolgellau. Infrequent buses from Machynlleth and Dolgellau.*

Parking: *As you approach the crossroad junction by Gwesty'r Llew Coch, cross the road to a car park near a play park on the opposite side.*

Going: *Moderate – woodland and hillside paths, tracks and lanes.*

Points of Interest:

[1] During the 15th and 16th centuries, Dinas Mawddwy was the territory of **Gwylliaid Cochion Mawddwy** (the *Red Bandits of Mawddwy*). Such was their notoriety, travellers crossed mountains on their journeys rather than take the road. Houses in the neighbourhood were built with a scythe-blade pointing skywards in the chimneys to deter the bandits from entering from the roofs. They were called Red Bandits

because most of them had red hair. They stole cattle and sheep and terrorised everyone. In 1554, Sir John Wynn of Gwydir and Baron Lewis Owen of Dolgellau were authorised to punish them. On Christmas Eve of that year they caught more than eighty of the bandits and all were condemned to death. The mother of two of them begged Baron Owen to spare the life of her youngest son. When he refused, she screamed and tore her blouse to reveal her breasts and said 'These breasts have given suck to those who shall wash their hands in your blood'. In the following year, Baron Owen was ambushed by the remaining bandits. All those with the baron fled except for his son-in-law, John Llwyd. It is said that the remaining sons of the old woman dipped their hands in his blood. After the baron's death the outlaws were completely exterminated. Dinas Mawddwy became an important centre for lead mining and slate quarrying.

[2] **Castell** is said to have a ghost. A woman who owned this farmhouse had an unfaithful husband. When she died, he forged her will using her dead hand. Later, the ghost of a hand was seen and there were other weird activities including furniture shaking and strange sounds.

[3] Over one hundred men worked at the **Minllyn slate quarry** before it closed about 1916. Tramways took the product to a mill on the valley floor. There are some interesting remains on the site, including the ruined mill, workshops, chimney and a tramway that goes through a tunnel to a pit.

[4] It is said that the Red Bandits of Mawddwy were buried near Collfryn, which is just over two kilometres south-east of this point. The lane on your left leads to Gweinion, and continues as a track and a right-of-way.

After fording a stream, it goes uphill to a fork. The left-hand track descends towards Collfryn. Before the cottage, at the eastern boundary of the wood on the left, is a large tree covered mound reputed to be the burial place of the bandits. Although not a right-of-way, use of the track is usually permitted to view the burial ground.

[5] **St Tydecho** was a missionary from Brittany and he founded a church on this site in the sixth century. The present building dates from the 14th century and has dormer windows at different levels. Inside are tiered pews and a barrel roof. Above the porch, dated 1641 are prehistoric animal bones which were dug up nearby about 1850. The **Brigands Inn** is said to have been the meeting place of the Red Bandits of Mawddwy. George Borrow stayed at the inn: he thought Mallwyd an attractive village.

The Brigands' Inn

[6] **Meirion Woollen Mill** is located in the old station of the former Mawddwy Railway. It ran from Cemaes Road (Glantwymyn) from 1868 to 1951. The coffee shop used to be the station master's house and booking office. Nearby is a 17th century double arched packhorse bridge known as Pont Minllyn.

Walk Directions: **[–] denotes Point of Interest**
1. From the Y Llew Coch (*The Red Lion*) in Dinas Mawddwy [1] take the minor road signposted Llanymawddwy. Walk downhill and in about 100 metres turn right on a clear track.

Y *Llew Coch, Dinas Mawddwy*

2. Cross a footbridge over Afon Dyfi and, with the river on your left, follow a path to a kissing gate. Immediately bear right and pass through a gap which once had a gate onto an enclosed track. After going through a wooden gate, bear right beside a fence. Pass through a metal gate and emerge on a track.

3. Turn right along the track and pass a house on the left. In about another 100 metres, where the track bears right, leave it to go ahead through a gate. Walk up to a footpath signpost then bear left to follow a fence on your left. Cross a stile into the wood and continue beside the fence. In about 15 metres turn right on a clear and steep path, uphill.

4. At the top of the wood climb over a stile and cross the field diagonally left. Go through trees to cross the field boundary and in about 10 metres follow an old river course to a stile in a fence on the left. Cross the stile then bear right along an old track. On reaching a corner, veer left on the track to have a wood on your right. As you climb higher there are lovely views across the Dyfi valley to Cwm Cywarch and the Aran Mountains.

5. Continue along the track and pass through a number of gates. After a left bend it descends to have

views of Cwm Cewydd on the right. Ignore the stile on your right. Continue ahead and go through another gate then, at the track junction, bear right to a metal gate. Pass farm buildings on your left  and a fantastic view of Cwm Cewydd on your right. Walk downhill to emerge on a lane.

6.   Turn right past Castell [2] and continue along the lane passing Fferm yr Hendre (or Hendref on the OS map) on your right. In 1.5 kilometres ignore an access lane on the right (Grid Ref. SH 872 136). Continue walking down the lane, crossing a bridge then to a lane junction. Turn left for a few metres then bear right on another lane that descends to the A458. Take care as you will now need to walk along the A458 which is a main road. At the junction, turn right and in about 50 metres cross a bridge over Afon Cleifion. Cross the road to a stile at the end of the bridge. Climb over the stile.

7.   Descend to walk along with the river on your left. In about 100 metres, leave the river to bear right uphill through trees to a field. Slant left to a fence but do not go through the metal gate which is ahead. With the fence on your left, walk uphill. After passing through more trees, continue uphill to a corner fence. Bear right and, at the end of the fence, join a track.

8.   Turn right along the track and follow it to a metal gate. From here you can look across the Dyfi valley to the remains of Minllyn quarry [3] above Coed Foeldinas. Emerge on an access lane [4] and bear right, downhill.

9. The lane descends to the A458. (A few metres to the right there is a cafe at the Murco garage.) Turn left to Brigands Inn and the roundabout with the A470. About 100 metres to the left stands the interesting 14th century church dedicated to St Tydecho [5]. At the roundabout, cross to the minor road opposite (second exit from A458) to Pont Mallwyd.

10. Follow the lane to Pont Mallwyd spanning Afon Dyfi. Ignore the footpath sign and stile on your left before crossing the bridge. Cross the bridge then turn left for about 100 metres. Immediately after passing the garden of a house called Bryn Ffynnon on your right, and opposite a track on your left, go through a gate on your right with the "Llwybr Cyhoeddus" (*Public Footpath*) sign.

11. Walk ahead on a track and follow it when it bears right to another gate. Walk uphill and, at a fork, ignore a track on the right. Continue uphill and at the next fork, bear right to cross a stream at a ford.

N.B. You may come across many pheasants along this path; this is due to a pheasant farm nearby. Take care when walking this trail as they do fly low in all directions.

12. Climb a ladder stile and, with the Dyfi valley below on your right, walk across the field. Descend slightly to a stile. With a fence on your right, walk ahead. This

field is known as Maes-y-Camlan, and is one of the many sites attributed to where King Arthur is said to have fought his last battle against Mordred.

13. At the end of the fence, pass through a gate. Immediately bear right to go through more gates and pass farm buildings on the right. Emerge on a lane and turn left.

14. In about 550 metres, after the lane crosses a stream, a path on the right leads to Meirion Mill [6]. Continue along the lane to the A470. If you visit the mill, leave by the exit onto the main road. Turn left along the A470 and continue for about 300 metres. Bear right along a road signposted for Dinas Mawddwy. It leads to the Gwesty'r Llew Coch (*The Red Lion*) and the start of the walk.

Facilities:
Refreshments at Gwesty'r Llew Coch, Mallwyd and Meirion Mill. Public toilets are opposite Gwesty'r Llew Coch at the start. Camp sites nearby.

Originally published in
Circular Walks in the Dyfi Valley

by Dorothy Hamilton

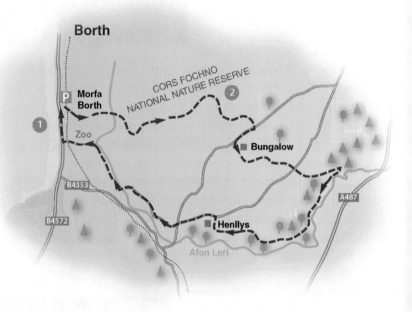

Walk 6
Borth – Pen-y-wern – Fron-goch – Afon Leri – Borth

Walk details

Approx distance: *8 miles/13 kilometres*

Approx time: *About 4 hours*

O.S. Maps: *1:50 000 Landranger Sheet 135*
1:25 000 Explorer OL 23

Start: *Borth sea front at the junction of the B4353 and B4572. Grid Ref. SN 608 890.*

Access: *Borth is north of Aberystwyth, 2½ miles (3.8 km) off the A487. Buses from Aberystwyth. Trains from Machynlleth and Aberystwyth.*

Parking: *Near roadside, Borth sea front.*

Going: *Moderate – field, woodland and riverside paths, tracks and lanes.*

Points of Interest:

[1] The attractive seaside resort of Borth was a small fishing village, until the arrival of the railway in 1863 brought visitors to the long sandy beach. Tree stumps of a submerged forest are uncovered on the shore at low tide. About halfway between Borth and Aberystwyth, the causeway called Sarn Gynfelyn stretches out for several miles into Cardigan Bay. According to legend, it is the remains of the lost lands of **Cantre'r Gwaelod**. Long ago, where Cardigan Bay is now, there was a fertile plain which had sixteen cities.

Sarn Gynfelyn

A system of dykes and sluices gave protection from the sea. In the 6th century, during the reign of Gwyddno Garanhir, the drunkard Seithennyn failed to carry out his job of closing the sluices. Cantre'r Gwaelod and all its peoples were drowned forever. Geological investigations have revealed that Cardigan Bay was once a plain, which was gradually encroached upon by the sea. This, however, probably took place at the end of the last Ice Age.

[2] The **National Nature Reserve of Cors Fochno** (*Borth bog*) is one of the best preserved lowland peat bogs in Britain. It was once much larger than it is now. Between 1820 and 1960, 1200 hectares of tidal marsh and bog were reclaimed and converted into farmland. Until the early 20th century, peat was cut from the edge of the bog and used as fuel by local people. According to legend, the bog was inhabited by a seven foot tall witch called Yr Hen Wrach (*The Old Witch*).

Cors Fochno

She got into people's houses and caused illness. Since Cors Fochno became a nature reserve, measures have been taken to help the bog retain its rainfall. This involves damming old ditches and channels.

The most important of the bog plants are the mosses and fourteen species occur in the reserve. Cotton grass, sundew and bog asphodel are some of the other plants that grow here. Otters are present. Birds include teal, curlew, reed bunting and skylark. Several uncommon species of moths have been found. A public footpath runs along the south edge of the reserve but to visit other parts, a permit is necessary. This can be obtained from the Ynys-las nature reserve centre.

Borth

Walk Directions: [–] **denotes Point of Interest**

1. At the junction of roads in Borth [1], if the tide is out, walk onto the beach and bear right. Alternatively, follow the B4353 in the direction of Ynys-las. If following the beach, leave it in approximately 900 metres, at the seventh long breakwater, and walk up the shingle to the road. At this point, there are no buildings on the seaward side of the road.

2. Take a narrow lane just before reaching Pebbles Bed and Breakfast. (There is a sign for St. Matthew's church.) Pass a chapel and bear right. Cross the railway line with care and walk in the direction of the church.

3. You are now walking on the Welsh Coastal Path.

Bear left to pass the church gates on your right. Go through two kissing gates and walk below a small hill. Follow a fence on the left. After going through another gate, go up to the embankment above Afon Leri.

4.   Bear right and in approximately 50 metres cross a footbridge over the river. Turn left and in a few metres leave the embankment to go through a kissing gate that is below on your right. In a few paces cross a footbridge over a channel. Follow the right boundary of the field to a signpost and turn left along the fence. Follow the fence to the gate of a farm. Although OS maps show that you may enter the farm, there are signs that say that you may not enter. Alternatively you will need to bear left to a metal gate ahead of you which leads to Pwll Du.

5.   Follow the waymarks for the Welsh Coastal Path to a Cors Fochno information sign [2]. Cross a stile then turn right to another stile. Follow the fence with a ford on your right then cross a stile with a stream on your left. Continue ahead to a farm.

6.   When you reach the top of the hill cross a stile and

turn left to continue walking down a tarmac lane with a farmhouse on your right. You are now leaving 'Cerrig-cyrannau Isaf' Farm. After going through a metal gate, bear right uphill then, after reaching the main road, turn right.

7.   Walk approximately 300 metres then turn left on a track towards a bungalow. Go through the gate ahead and walk across the field to find a stile near the top left-hand corner.

8.   Follow an old track between trees and go through a gate. Continue along the edge of the field. Bear slightly left to a stile below the farm. Go ahead to a stile.

9.   Follow the right-hand boundary of the field around two sides. Walk towards the telegraph poles and bear left to a stile. Cross a stile and walk along the right side of this field to a stile at a corner. Pass buildings on the left and follow the hedge to two stiles and a lane.

10. Turn left and in just over 100 metres, cross a stile on the right. Walk ahead, uphill, along the right boundaries of fields. Descend to the edge of a wood and cross a stile. Follow the path that slants to the left, downhill, through coniferous trees.

11. Emerge on a wider track, where there is a barrier on the left. Ignore the path straight ahead (which leads to Talybont) and turn a sharp right.

12. Stay on the wide trail all

the way to a gate at the edge of the forest. Ignore all other paths and trails when walking through the forest.

13. After reaching the gate, cross the field by going slightly uphill to join a track that passes between trees and gorse. Continue ahead and pass the ruined farmhouse called Fron-goch on your right. Walk uphill to the top left-hand boundary of the field and pass through a gate in the corner into the next field.

14. Bear left into another field. Cross, descending slightly, towards the far left corner. Pass a fence on the right and trees on the left to find a stile near a bridle gate. Walk ahead uphill and bear right to pass behind a farmhouse. Leave the next field by going through a gate on the left.

15. Turn right on the track to emerge on a lane. Turn left and, after passing a house on the right, reach a lane junction. Bear left around a bend and, in approximately 30 metres, turn right on a narrow lane.

16. Pass a farm on the right and turn left at a junction. At the end of the lane bear left into some trees. Cross a footbridge over Afon Leri and immediately turn right on a footpath. Pass a caravan site on the left. Go through a kissing gate and walk ahead with the river on your right.

17. Pass through another kissing gate to have a track parallel to the path. On reaching the lane to the Animalarium, bear left to follow it towards Borth.

Cross the railway at the level crossing and reach the B4353 in Borth. Turn left to return to the start of the walk.

Facilities:
Refreshments in Borth. Public toilets near the start of the walk. Animalarium. Several campsites in the area.

Originally published in
Circular Walks in the Dyfi Valley

by Dorothy Hamilton

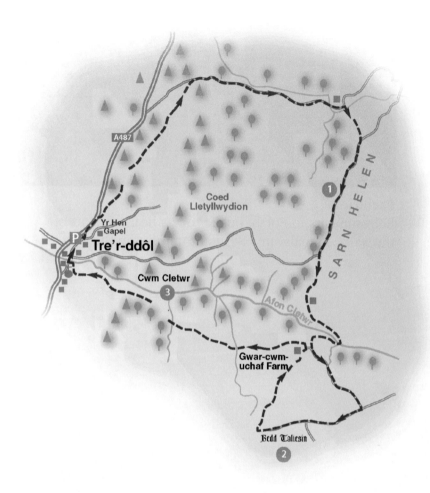

Coed
Lletyllwydion

A487

SARN HELEN

Yr Hen
Gapel
Tre'r-ddôl

Cwm Cletwr

Afon Cletwr

**Gwar-cwm-
uchaf Farm**

Bedd Taliesin

Walk 7
Tre'r-ddôl – Sarn Helen – Bedd Taliesin
– Tre'r-ddôl

Walk details

Approx distance: *4 ¾ miles/7.6 kilometres*

Approx time: *3 – 3½ hours*

O.S. Maps: *1:50 000 Landranger Sheet 135*
1:25 000 Explorer OL 23

Start: *Siop Cynfelyn at Cletwr, Tre'r-ddôl.*
Grid Ref. SN 660 923

Access: *Tre'r-ddôl is off the A487, 8½ miles (13.5 km) south of Machynlleth. Buses from Machynlleth and Aberystwyth pass through Tre'r-ddôl. When approaching the sign for Tre'r-ddol from Machynlleth, in about 300 metres take the left exit to enter the village then turn immediately right to the shop car park.*

Parking: *Siop Cynfelyn at Cletwr car park (no charge).*

Going: *Moderate – woodland and field paths, tracks and lanes.*

Points of Interest:

[1] **Sarn Helen** is a Roman Road linking the forts between Caerhun, near Conwy, and *Moridunum* at Caerfyrddin (Carmarthen). Sarn means road and, according to tradition, it was named after the wife of the Roman Emperor, Macsen Wledig (Magnus Maximus). According to the story in Y *Mabinogion*, the Emperor dreamt of a lady in a far off land. When he

woke up he remembered his dream and sent messengers around the world to look for her. After searching for a long time, they found Elen at Aber Saint, near Caernarfon. The emperor came to Wales and married Elen and, at her request, built a road linking south and north Wales – hence Sarn Helen. The remains of the Bryndyfi lead mines are located about 200 metres north-east of the lane junction. At the end of the 19th century, about one hundred men worked in the mines, but they closed after about two years as only a small amount of lead ore was found.

[2] **Bedd Taliesin** is a Bronze Age cairn dating from about 2,000 BC. In the centre there is a two metre

long grave where, according to rumour, a skull was once found. The cairn is reputed to contain the bones of Taliesin, the 6th century Welsh poet, greatest of all bards. Legend has it that he was found as a baby in a coracle caught on a fishing weir near Borth by Elffin, the son of Gwyddno Garanhir. When Taliesin grew up he rescued Elffin from a dungeon in Deganwy castle.

[3]   **Cwm Cletwr** is a Site of Special Scientific Interest. The 52 acre nature reserve consists of sessile oak and ash woodlands, with a wide variety of mosses and lichens. Flowers include yellow archangel, dog's mercury and woodruff. Look out for dippers and woodpeckers.

Walk Directions: **[–] denotes Point of Interest**

1.   Exit Siop Cynfelyn car park, turn left and follow the road to the A487. Before arriving at the junction, on your right is Yr Hen Gapel (*The Old Chapel*) which has a commemorative plaque inscribed with information about its significance:

> *"In this chapel began the religious revival of 1859 which had a powerful impact throughout Wales and beyond. Its first leader was Humphrey Jones (1832-1895), who was born and brought up in this village before emigrating to Wisconsin."*

Turn right and, in approximately 100 metres (just before a lay-by) bear right at a footpath signpost to follow a path into woodland.

2.   When the path forks, bear left and walk uphill to meet a forest track. Continue straight ahead and follow it to a lane. Bear right along this quiet lane. After a kilometre you will reach Cefngweiriog Farm. To the right side of the farmhouse is a footpath signpost directing to a wooden gate. Go through this gate and cross the field in a south-easterly direction towards a metal gate and a footpath signpost. The gate leads to the Roman Road, Sarn Helen [1].

3.   Turn right and walk down the lane for about 780 metres to a junction. Ignore the lane on the right. Descend through trees to a bridge across Afon Cletwr. Walk uphill on the lane and, before reaching the farm

buildings of Gwar-cwm-uchaf, turn left on a clear track with a footpath signpost.

4.   The track passes between fields and follows a stream on the left. In about 600 metres it joins another track. From here, there are fine views of the Dyfi estuary.

5.   Turn right along the firm track. Go through a gate across it and, a few metres before reaching a lane, you will see Bedd Taliesin [2] on your left (GR: SN 671 912).

6.   Walk ahead to join the lane and turn right. Go through a gate and follow the lane as far as Gwar-cwm-uchaf.

7.   After passing the house, and before reaching other

buildings, find the footpath signpost and bear left to go through a gate. Pass the house on your left and follow a track. Go through a gate and cross a stream. Continue beside a left-hand fence and pass through a small patch of woodland.

8.   Go through a small gate to pass above a stream. Follow a fence on the right but, when it bears right, walk ahead across the field.

9.   Join a track and go through a gate across it. Continue on the track, which gives fine views of the surrounding countryside and Dyfi estuary. Enter a wood and descend on a clear path that bends right and left. On reaching a gate, ignore the steep descending path beside it.

10. Go through the gate and continue on a path through coniferous trees. Pass through more gates and join another path above Afon Cletwr. Turn right if you wish to explore Cwm Cletwr Nature Reserve [3].

11. Return along the path to have the river on your right. Descend to a track and follow it to the road in Tre'r-ddôl. Turn right and cross the bridge to return to the start of the walk.

Facilities:

Refreshments at The Wild Fowler Inn or Siop Cynfelyn.

Originally published in
Circular Walks in the Dyfi Valley

by Dorothy Hamilton

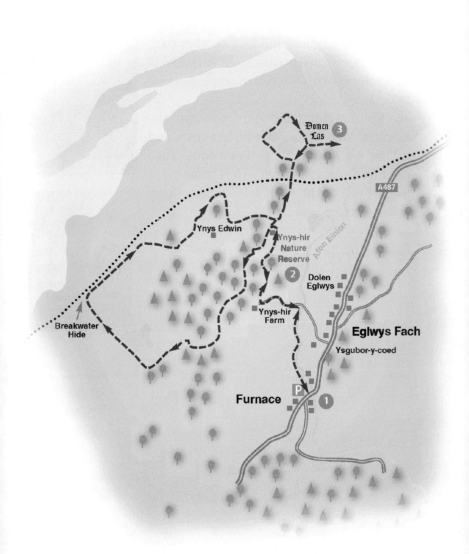

Domen
Las 3

Ynys Edwin

A487

Ynys-hir
Nature
Reserve

Afon Einion

2

Dolen
Eglwys

Ynys-hir
Farm

Eglwys Fach

Breakwater
Hide

Ysgubor-y-coed

P

1

Furnace

Walk 8

Ffwrnais (*Furnace*) – Ynys-hir – Domen Las – Ffwrnais

Walk details

Approx distance: *6 miles/9.5 kilometres*

Approx time: *3½ – 4 hours*

O.S. Maps: *1:50 000 Landranger Sheet 135*
1:25 000 Explorer OL 23.

Start: *Dyfi Furnace (Cadw monument) in the village of Furnace. Grid Ref. SN 685952.*

Access: *Furnace is on the A487, 7 miles (11 km) south-west of Machynlleth. Buses from Aberystwyth and Machynlleth.*

Parking: *Car park along surfaced track opposite the Dyfi Furnace*

Going: *Easy/Moderate – Paths, tracks and lane. Most of the walk is through a nature reserve – dogs not allowed – for which there is a charge (unless you are a RSPB member).*

Points of Interest:

[1] The name **Furnace** comes from the impressive monument next to the waterfall on Afon Einion. The blast furnace was built as part of an ironworks in about 1755 by Jonathan Kendall from Staffordshire. Iron ore was shipped from Cumberland to a nearby port on Afon Dyfi. Charcoal produced from local deciduous woods provided fuel for the furnace. A channel was built to carry water from Afon Einion to the water-

wheel that powered the bellows. The blast provided the high temperatures necessary to smelt iron. Dyfi Furnace was in use for about fifty years. After being abandoned the building was taken over as a sawmill. The water-wheel dates from that period of time.

[2] **Ynys-hir** RSPB nature reserve comprises a wide

range of habitats covering over 1000 acres. The ancient oak woodlands support pied flycatchers, wood warblers, redstarts, nuthatches, tree creepers and woodpeckers. In spring there is a carpet of bluebells and wood anemones. Goldcrest may be spotted in the coniferous trees, whilst water rails and warblers breed in the reedbeds. The saltmarshes attract numerous wildfowl, including widgeon, mallard, teal, tufted duck, shoveller and red-breasted merganser. Sundew, bog asphodel and bog rosemary grow in the peat bogs. Birds of prey such as

red kite, buzzard and peregrine hunt over the marshes. Many species of butterflies and moths have been found on the reserve, including several uncommon species.

[3] Herons nest at **Domen Las** and the path, hide and motte and bailey castle are not accessible during the breeding season. The motte stands on a rocky ridge overlooking the Dyfi estuary. It was probably built in 1156 by Rhys ap Gruffudd, as a defence against Owain Gwynedd. A few years later it was taken by the Norman lord, Roger de Clare. He rebuilt the castle, but shortly afterwards, Rhys recaptured it.

Walk Directions:
[–] **denotes Point of Interest**
1.   At the Dyfi Furnace [1] cross the road to the surfaced track opposite. Pass a car park on the right and walk ahead with Afon Einion on the right. Pass a bungalow on the left and  continue along the track to emerge on a lane.

2.   Turn left and pass the drive to Ynys-hir Hall. In about 150 metres bear right to follow the signs for the RSPB Ynys-hir nature reserve [2].

3.   To enter the reserve you must pay a small entrance fee at the reception centre. After leaving the reception, follow a path to a small gate. Turn left on a broad track. In about 100 metres, at a small pond on the left, turn right to a wooden gate then bear left at a fork. Continue along a  path through woodland to the Ynys-hir hide.

4.   Pass the hide on your right and continue along the path to a grassy track and wooden gate.

Turn left then go through another wooden gate to cross a track to another path with a metal gate and a purple arrow on it. After crossing a couple of footbridges and passing through reed beds, you will reach the Covert Du hide.

5. Continue along the path and pass the Ynys Eidiol hide. Cross a footbridge and go through a gate to emerge on a track. Cross to a stile and follow a path to the Breakwater hide.

6. Pass the hide on your left and continue along the path. Cross a stile and walk along with the railway line on your left. Cross a footbridge on your right and walk away from the railway line.

7. On reaching a fork, turn right along the track and cross a stile at a gate. In about 40 metres, leave the main track to bear left. A path on the right leads to the top of a small hill, a fine viewpoint with a bench.

8. Return the same way down the hill and walk ahead to a small gate. Follow a board walk through trees and emerge on a broad track. Turn left and, when there is a gate ahead, bear right on a path to have a fence on your left.

9. When the path enters woodland, bear left and ignore a path on the right. Emerge on a track and turn right. In a few metres, at a junction, bear left on a wide track. Go through a gate and cross a bridge over the railway line. Go through a small gate on the left and in a few paces, at a fork, take the left-hand path.

10. Pass a pool on the left. Go through a small gate on the left and cross a footbridge. Continue along the

path and pass the Saltings hide on your right. The path bears right to a stile. The stile and path on the left leads to Domen Las (closed February – July) [3].

11. Return to the main path. From here you can walk uphill to the Marian Mawr hide. Continue along the path to have a fence on the left. On reaching a path junction, bear left to cross the railway bridge and return along the track to the junction met earlier.

12. Walk ahead and go through a gate. In a few paccs, bear left to return to the reception centre. Retrace your steps to the start at Furnace.

Facilities:
Alternative parking, refreshments and toilets at Ynys-hir Nature Reserve.

Originally published in
Circular Walks in the Dyfi Valley

by Dorothy Hamilton

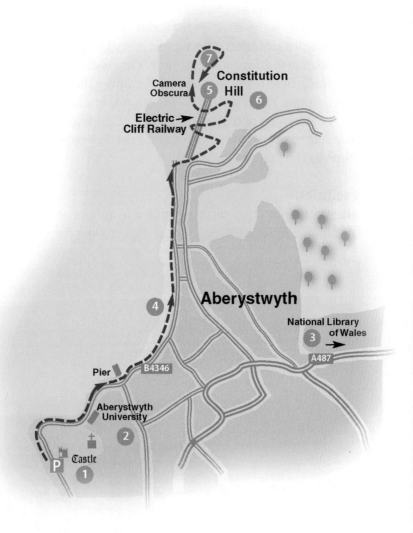

Walk 9
Aberystwyth – up Constitution Hill

Walk details

Approx distance: *4 miles/6.5 kilometres*

Approx time: *2 – 2½ hours*

O.S. Maps: *1:50 000 Landranger Sheet 135*
1:25 000 Explorer OL 213

Start: *Aberystwyth Castle*
Grid Ref. SN 579 815

Access: *Aberystwyth is the major town of Ceredigion,*
served by the A487, A44, A4120 and A485 main
roads, and also by train.

Parking: *There are numerous options in the town. Parking is*
available close to the castle, along the promenade as
well as at the nearby harbour.

Going: *Easy – Moderate. Gentle stroll along the promenade*
then a fairly challenging walk up Constitution Hill.
Plenty of viewpoint stops along the way.

Points of Interest:

[1] **Aberystwyth Castle** The first castle at
Aberystwyth was a Norman motte and bailey built by
Gilbert de Clare "Strongbow" in about 1109, an early
incursion of a Norman baron into Wales securing the
headland close to Llanbadarn, one of the spiritual
centres of Wales. Gilbert presumably did not hold the
castle long for it was in the hands of Cadwaladr, a son
of Gruffudd ap Cynan, in 1143 when in a petty dispute
with Anarawd, son of Gruffudd ap Rhys of Deheubarth,

 he killed Anarawd. At the time Anarawd was set to marry one of the daughters of Owain Gwynedd. Owain was Cadwaladr's brother and ruler of Gwynedd, the marriage allowing him to expand his sphere of influence to include Deheubarth and so, hopefully and eventually, to unify Wales against the Normans. Faced with a choice between supporting his brother of continuing with his political ends, Owain chose the latter forcing his brother into exile. One of his first acts was to take Cadwaladr's main castle, here at Aberystwyth.

The first castle would have been of wood, with defensive earthworks, but as part of Edward I's 'Ring of Stone' built after his campaigns of the late 13th century, that early structure was replaced with one in stone. As with all of Edward's castles, Aberystwyth could be supplied by sea – the Welsh could lay siege, but with a sea-gate the castle could hold out indefinitely.

Edward's castle remained a Norman stronghold for over a century until it was captured by the Welsh during the struggles of Owain Glyndŵr. In 1404 Glyndŵr controlled almost all of Wales, his position being so secure that he could turn his attention to the great castles. In quick succession Harlech, Cricieth and Aberystwyth were taken by his forces. Although he used Harlech as his main stronghold Aberystwyth was important, standing at the border between the north, which would always follow him, and the south which, historically, had been under Norman rule and so needed to be watched. By 1407 Owain's position was in decline and his forces in retreat. During the summer Prince Henry – the Monmouth-born son of Henry IV, a young man who would become the legendary Henry V – arrived at the castle walls with an army and the newest weapon in the king's armoury, cannons. There were seven cannons in all, including a 4½ ton monster called the King's Gonne and another called, with the gallows humour of the military, The Messenger. With the cannon came five hundredweight of powder, nine hundredweight of saltpetre and three hundredweight of sulphur. The castle garrison, used to siege engines but never having seen a cannon, were terrified by the initial bombardment. But equally fearful were the cannoniers: medieval cannon were notoriously dangerous and one at the siege exploded killing everyone close to it.

But, despite the cannon, the castle held out. By September both sides were weary, and the castle commander, Rhys Ddu, took advantage of this to offer Prince Henry a deal. He suggested a truce until 24th October at which point fighting would resume for a week. If by 1st November the castle had not been relieved Rhys would surrender it. Prince Henry accepted, a treaty was signed and the Prince's army retreated to Strata Florida for a rest. Owain Glyndŵr took his chance to resupply and reinforce the castle.

The understandably annoyed Prince Henry returned laying siege through a savage winter that saw snow blanket the whole of Wales from Christmas until March. With dwindling supplies the castle garrison waited for the thaw and relief, but Owain was not in a position to resupply by sea and his tenuous hold on the countryside meant he could not resupply by land either. By late 1408 the situation was hopeless and the castle surrendered.

Much later the castle was used as a mint with silver from local lead mines being used for the coinage, but the building was then abandoned to the elements. Today only the remains of a few walls and one round tower remain.

[2] The Old College – Aberystwyth University

During his period of power Owain held a parliament at Machynlleth, to the north of Aberystwyth, at which he outlined his vision of a Wales free of English domination. One of his aims was to create a university so that an educated generation of the Welsh could organise the country's own affairs. It is ironic, therefore, that within a few seconds' walk from the castle that was one of Glyndŵr's main strongholds that there is a college of the Aberystwyth University. In the 1860s Thomas Savin, builder of the Cambrian Coast railway line, built a hotel at Aberystwyth with the idea of selling a package from London's Euston which included return rail fare and nights at a quality hotel. The venture failed and in 1870 the derelict hotel was bought by a group of Welshman with the intention of creating a new college of the University of Wales. The new college opened in 1872 with just 26 students. For 10 years the college was maintained by voluntary fund raising, but then the Government was persuaded to grant finance. After 135 years as University College of Wales Aberystwyth, in 2007 it became an independent university in its own right by becoming Aberystwyth University. The University has expanded, both in terms of buildings and student numbers, and in reputation: the Departments of International Politics, Geography and the Institute of Biological and Rural Sciences are world renowned.

Many of the University's buildings lie on Penglais Hill up which the A487 exits Aberystwyth. Several of the students' halls of residence occupy old hotels on the sea front.

[3] **National Library of Wales** One of the most impressive buildings on Penglais hill houses the National Library of Wales, established by a charter of Edward VII in 1907. The idea was put forward in 1873 but, as with many things in and concerning Wales, it took several decades of campaigning for the idea to come to fruition. (The university idea took 470 years.) Under the Copyright Act of 1911, the Library is entitled to a copy of all books, pamphlets, maps etc. published in the United Kingdom. The library has the first book to be published in Welsh and the first to have been published in Wales, as well as many priceless medieval manuscripts.

[4] **Aberystwyth Seafront** From the southern end of the sea-front promenade, Aberystwyth reveals itself as the archetypal Victorian sea-side resort; the beach to the left just beyond the pier, and to the right an array

of elegant houses, many of them once hotels. Once known as the 'Biarritz of Wales' the town claimed to be the possessor of many sunshine and temperature records for Britain, and to have the most temperate winters of any British resort. The town is now home to the largest Arts Centre in Wales and the Ceredigion Museum (next to the Tourist Information Office in Terrace Road), which explores the history of the county. The museum is housed in a former theatre and has been described as 'probably the most beautiful museum in Britain'.

[5] **Electric Cliff Railway** The Electric Cliff Railway

was built in 1896 by George Croydon Marks, who was also partly responsible for the pier at the other end of the sea front. Engineered to allow holidaymakers to enjoy the view and to take a constitution at the top of the hill, the funicular was

originally powered by gravity, a water tank on the descending train being filled so that its weight hauled the ascending train up. At the bottom the tank was emptied into the sea. Only later were the electric motors that give the railway its name installed. The track is 237m (778ft) long, the longest in Britain. The funicular runs only during the holiday season.

[6] **Constitution Hill** Constitution Hill is named for

the walks taken by Victorian seasiders as part of their Aberystwyth holiday or rest cure. The walkers were also entertained by a standard series of amusements in 'Luna Park' – bandstand, ballroom, camera obscura (see point 7) and even an early roller coaster.

The view from the hill is impressive and explains the importance of Aberystwyth's site. Between the hill and Pen Dinas to the south is a small, but well-sheltered, bay into which Afon Ystwyth flows, a naturally strategic site. Pen Dinas is topped by an Iron Age hill-fort on which stands the Wellington Monument, erected in 1852 to commemorate the Iron Duke's victory at Waterloo in 1815.

[7] **Camera Obscura** The Camera Obscura was built in Victorian times for the delight and amusement of the holidaymakers. The original version was housed a short distance from the present building, which was erected in 1985 with a new 14 inch (35 cm) lens (then the biggest in the world). Using a mirror at the top of the building and the lens a view of the surrounding countryside is projected on to the viewing table. It is said that a clear image of 2,500 square kilometres (1,000 square miles) of country surrounding Aberystwyth can be seen in good weather. Close to the Camera Obscura is

Y Consti Restaurant which offers breathtaking views of Aberystwyth and Cardigan Bay. It is situated where the former Summerhouse Tearooms were, and built at about the same time as the funicular, making them (probably) once, the oldest cafe in town.

Walk Directions:

[–] **denotes Point of Interest**

1. From the castle [1] head towards the seafront promenade, soon passing the Old College of Aberystwyth University [2] to the right. The pier is soon reached. It was built in 1864, but refurbished in 1896 and again in 1922. It is 213m (700ft) long. From close to the pier there is an impressive view of Aberystwyth's seafront [4].

2. Continue along the seafront, either by walking along the promenade above the beach or by walking along the beach itself. At the far end of the seafront is the lower station of the Cliff Railway [4]. There is now a choice: either take the railway or climb the steep path to the top of Constitution Hill [6].

3. The path – or, rather,

one of the paths as there is quite a complex, just keep going up – crosses the railway a couple of times, eventually reaching the top station with its gift shop etc. Close by is the Camera Obscura [7].

4. From the summit of Constitution Hill the walk can be extended to any length by following the cliff path northwards to Clarach, or even on to Borth (about 6 miles/9.5 kilometres). Alternatively, return to the castle by detouring through the town.

Refreshments
Every taste and pocket is catered for in Aberystwyth.

Originally published in
Ceredigion Walks

by Richard Sale

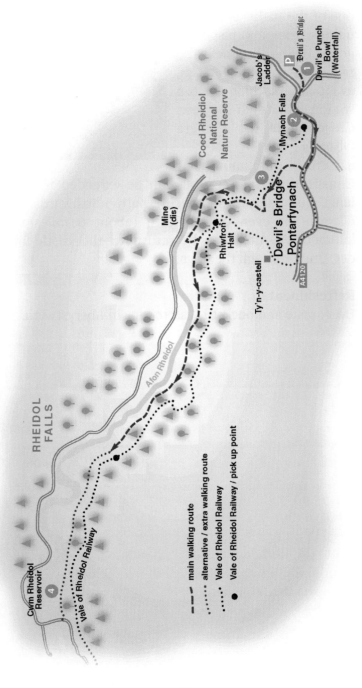

Devil's Punch
Bowl (Waterfall)

Devil's Bridge

Jacob's
Ladder

Coed Rheidiol
National
Nature Reserve

Mynach Falls

Devil's Bridge
Pontarfynach

A4120

Mine
(dis)

Rhiwfron
Halt

Ty'n-y-castell

Afon Rheidol

RHEIDOL
FALLS

Cwm Rheidol
Reservoir

Vale of Rheidol Railway

- - - main walking route
· · · · · alternative / extra walking route
——— Vale of Rheidol Railway
● Vale of Rheidol Railway / pick up point

Walk 10
Pontarfynach – cross the Devil's Bridge

Walk details

Approx distance: *4 miles/6.5 kilometres*

Approx time: 2½-3 hours

O.S. Maps: *1:50 000 Landranger Sheet 135*
                 1:25 000 Explorer OL 213

Start: *Pontarfynach (Devil's Bridge)*
                 Grid Ref. SN 741 770

Access: *Pontarfynach (Devil's Bridge) lies on the A4120,*
                 the road which rises through Cwm Rheidol from
                 Aberystwyth to Ponterwyd, where it links with the
                 A44. Pontarfynach can also be reached from
                 Aberystwyth by the Vale of Rheidol railway and
                 several buses.

Parking: *There is a car park close to the famous falls, and at*
                 the Vale of Rheidol railway terminus.
                 Grid Ref. SN 743 771

Going: *Moderate. Though short, the walk has one sharp*
                 climb (unless the railway option is used).

Ideally a walk around the *Devil's Bridge* falls would be offered, but crossing points of Afon Rheidol are limited, and all such walks involve a section of main road. This walk minimises road walking, and also has an option of using the Vale of Rheidol Railway so as to eliminate roads altogether.

Points of Interest:

[1] Despite being associated with beautiful Cwm Rheidiol the triple bridges of **Devil's Bridge** do not

actually cross Afon Rheidol. The river below is the Afon Mynach, the monk's river, named for the monks of the abbey at Strata Florida who owned sheep grazing land in the area. It was the monks who built the first bridge – the lower one of course! – in 1087 and it was called Pontarfynach (the Monk's Bridge), which is still the Welsh name for the hamlet. The English name is a translation of Pont-y-gŵr-drwg, literally the bridge of the Evil One, the name deriving from a legend about the method of construction of the first bridge. The legend concerns Marged, an old woman who lived alone close to the edge of the ravine making a living by selling the milk of Malen, her only cow. One morning, after a night of torrential rain, Marged went out to milk Malen but discovered that before the rain had started the cow had crossed the stream, and was now marooned on the far side by a raging torrent. Marged was in despair – if she did not milk Malen not only would there be no milk to sell but the cow would also suffer. What would happen to Marged if the cow died? Marged wrung her hands and shouted loudly that she would give anything for a bridge to cross the stream. To her astonishment a man's voice answered saying that he would build her a bridge and, looking across the ravine, she saw a figure in the distinctive white habit and cowl of a Strata Florida monk. Marged could not see his face, and the cowl seemed oddly shaped,

70

but so desperate was she that the details did not really register. Neither did the fact that she could clearly hear the stranger over the rush of the water below. Marged asked how long the bridge would take and the stranger replied about an hour, but that she must not watch the work. She agreed, hurrying back to her cottage so quickly that she failed to notice the significance of the stranger's final remark, that he must be allowed to take the first living thing which crossed the bridge.

After an hour of anxious waiting Marged returned to find the bridge in place, but as she started to cross she saw that the monk's cowl had slipped slightly, revealing the reason for the curious shape – the stranger had horns, it was the Devil in disguise. Now Marged recalled his final sentence and realised that she would forfeit her soul if she crossed. She hesitated and stared at the bridge. The impatient Devil asked her what the problem was and she replied that the bridge did not look secure, in fact it did not seem strong enough to bear the weight of the crust of bread she was carrying, a morsel from her breakfast. The exasperated Devil said that to test the bridge she should throw the crust on to it, but Marged threw the crust right across the bridge and her dog immediately scampered after it, becoming the first living thing to cross. The furious Devil disappeared in a cloud of sulphurous smoke, but the bridge remained intact allowing Marged to be re-united with Malen and her dog.

The triple bridges are an object lesson in the advance of bridge building techniques. As span lengths could be increased the bridges moved nearer to the top of the ravine.

[2] Beneath the bridges are the **Mynach Falls** and the **Devil's Punchbowl**, superbly natural creations, access

to which is strictly controlled and by payment only. Most walkers will have mixed feelings about this; on the debit side, how can anyone charge for such a natural phenomenon? On the other hand we live in a country where, rightly or wrongly, all land is privately owned (even common and open-access land) and the owners do maintain the paths and steps, for the benefit of everyone.

Glimpses of the beauty spots can be obtained from the bridge and road edges, but to explore them thoroughly the site must be visited. It is very worthwhile – this really is a very beautiful gorge, one of the best natural scenes in Ceredigion if not the whole of Wales. The Punchbowl lies on the southern side of the bridges, a smooth hollow in the bedrock of the stream caused by millennia of scouring by pebbles carried by the rushing water. To the north of the bridge are the Falls and some marvellous woodland. To experience the best of them it is necessary to descend almost 100m (300ft) to the river, reaching a point close to the confluence of Afon Mynach and Afon Rheidol.

It almost seems so self-evident that this site is beautiful that it comes as a surprise to find that George Barrow, that intrepid mid-19th century traveller whose book *Wild Wales* has become such a classic, did not share the opinion. Barrow stayed at the Hafod Arms Hotel, the 'immense lofty cottage with projecting eaves' which still stands. Borrow viewed the scene below the bridges with the awe-struck horror that seemed to be the requirement of visitors of the period. The Punchbowl was 'a frightful cavity (where) the waters . . . whirl, boil and hiss in a horrid pot or cauldron . . . in a manner truly tremendous'. The waters then escape through 'a gloomy volcanic slit'. Borrow suggested that, after seeing the Punchbowl (which he called by the local name of Twll yn y Graig) and the 'spectral, shadowy Devil's Bridge', you should 'repair to your inn, and have no more sight-seeing that day, for you have seen enough!' Neither could he come to terms with the falls themselves which were 'thundering beside you; foam, foam, foam is flying all about you; the basin . . . is boiling frightfully below you', together with 'rocks . . . frowning terribly on you' and 'forest trees, dank and wet with spray and mist'. It would be interesting to find out if Borrow really did find it so bad, or whether his intended audience coloured his perception. For the modern walker it is all of these horrid, frightful things that are so attractive.

Borrow does not mention the legend of Marged and the Devil, but he does mention a story centred on a cave, now no longer visible as such, at the base of the falls. Here, he says, lived the Plant de Bat, or children of Bat, a local man. They, two boys and a girl, were notorious locally as petty thieves. One day they killed a gentleman while robbing him, and his friends sought them out, destroying the cave so they could no longer use it. The boys were hanged and the girl burnt at the stake.

[3] The **Vale of Rheidol Railway** opened in 1902, chiefly to transport the ore from the lead mines of Cwm Rheidol, which were dotted along the upper

valley from Aberffrwd to Pontarfynach, though the line also carried timber and passengers. The awkward terrain, and the usual desire to save money, meant that a narrow gauge track was laid. The last of the mines closed around the time of the 1914–18 War after which the line became one of the major tourist attractions of Aberystwyth, coaches from Pontarfynach taking visitors to see Pumlumon. The line was taken over by Great Western Railways in 1922 and was the last steam service to be operated by British Rail. In 1989 it was taken over by the Brecon Mountain Railway Co. and is now operated as one of the 'Great Little Trains of Wales'. The journey from Devil's Bridge to Aberystwyth (or vice versa) takes an hour.

[4] Just beyond the pretty Rheidol Falls the valley has been flooded to create the **Cwm Rheidol Reservoir**. At its head, close to the Falls, is a hydro-electric power station operated by PowerGen. The station and its fish farm can be visited, and there is also an information centre.

Walk Directions:

[–] denotes Point of Interest

1. From Pontarfynach (Devil's Bridge) [1] and the entrance to the natural scenery of Afon Mynach [2], follow the A4120, with care, past the Hafod Arms Hotel.

2. Continue past the terminus of the Vale of Rheidol railway [3] and through the

hamlet of Devil's Bridge/ Pontarfynach. Walk past two houses to the right, Llys Maeth and Fronhaul, turning right beyond on the latter. The footpath sign and gate is found just before  the speed limit signs at the edge of the hamlet. The path heads north, soon reaching woodland beside the railway.

3.   Follow the signpost and ignore the grassy path on the right to a gate by the railway. Continue walking to a wooden gate by the railway and follow the path slightly uphill to woodland. Follow the path to a footbridge. Take care as the path can be rather muddy and slippery.

4.   The path soon reaches the railway. Cross, with care, and continue, now walking close to the line. Eventually the path drops away from the line, falling steeply as it sweeps in a gentle leftward curve towards Afon Rheidol. You have entered the Cwm Rheidol National Nature Reserve. The mixed, but chiefly conifer, wood, here is superb and excellent for woodland birds.

5.   When you reach a metal gate and forest information sign at the edge of the forest, turn left up the steep hill. The path will eventually reach a T-junction of paths.

6.   There is a choice here. Turning right

allows a clear path to be followed to the Rheidol Falls [4] and the nearby railway station. From there the train can be taken back to Pontarfynach. This has the advantage of a ride on the train, a relaxing return, and the avoidance of the short section of walking on the A4120. The disadvantage, of course, is the need to time your arrival to a train's departure.

7.   To return by foot, turn left, following the path (it is actually a bridleway) across the railway again (close to the Rhiwfren Station). Beyond, the path continues through woodland, then beside fences to Ty'n-y-Castell Farm. Now take the farm access lane to reach the A4120.

8.   Turn left and follow the road, with care, back to Pontarfynach.

Refreshments
There are several possibilities at Pontarfynach.

Originally published in
Ceredigion Walks

by Richard Sale

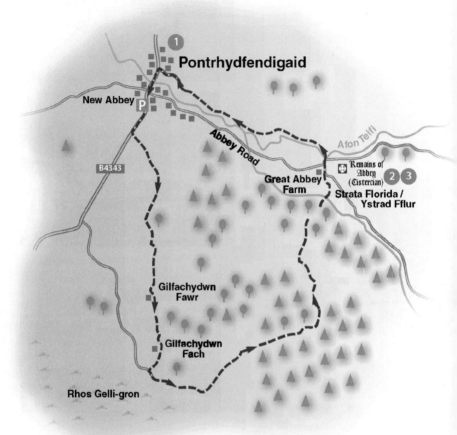

Walk 11
Ystrad Fflur – the beautiful ruins of Strata Florida

Walk details

Approx distance: *5½ miles/9 kilometres*

Approx time: 4 hours

O.S. Maps: *1:50 000 Landranger Sheet 147*
                   1:25 000 Explorer OL 187

Start: *Pontrhydfendigaid. Grid Ref. SN 728 660*

Access: *Pontrhydfendigaid lies at the junction of the B4343*
                   which links Tregaron to Pontarfynach and the
                   B4340 which heads north-westwards to
                   Aberystwyth. Pontrhydfendigaid can be reached
                   from Aberystwyth by the T21 bus to Tregaron.

Parking: *Parking is available, with care, in the village, but is*
                   easier in a large layby beside the B4343 to the south
                   of the village, and on the route (GR: SN 729 662).
                   There is also good parking at the Ystrad Fflur abbey
                   site but this is strictly reserved for visitors to the
                   ruins.

Going: *Difficult. The walk is long and poorly way-marked*
                   and care must be taken with route findings. The
                   walk directions reflect this, being very exact: please
                   study them carefully.

Points of Interest:

[1] The village of **Pontrhydfendigaid** is named for the *pont* (bridge) built across Afon Teifi so that those approaching Ystrad Fflur (*Strata Florida*) would not

have to use the *rhyd fendigaid* (*the blessed ford*). It is a straggling, but likeable, place with a good cafe and inn. [2] **Strata Florida** is the Latin form of the Welsh **Ystrad Fflur**, the valley of Afon Fflur that also runs into Cors Caron, parallel to, but 2 miles (3.5 kilometres) south of, Afon Teifi. The reason is that the abbey was originally sited 2 miles (3.5 kilometres) to the south-west in a field that is still called Yr Hen Fynachlog (the old monastery). The founding of the abbey is generally ascribed to Robert FitzStephen who held large tracts of West Wales, and the agreed date is around 1160, some 100 years after the Conquest. The benefaction, so far into Wales, was fraught with danger: within two years Rhys ap Gruffudd had attacked the local Norman strongholds and taken FitzStephen prisoner.

The abbey that FitzStephen had founded was Cisterican, an order which extolled the virtues of simplicity, hard work in agriculture, and extreme poverty. It seems that the quiet dignity of the house won Rhys over, a character of 1184 naming him as the builder of the abbey. Though some work may have been carried out during his rule of Ceredigion, the building of Ystrad Fflur occupied a very long period, the Chapter House having been completed only in 1235, and the bell only being bought in 1254. The cost of the bell was 97 marks and two cows.

Despite its Norman foundations the abbey became, perhaps because of its remoteness from England, a great centre for Welsh culture and an influential voice in Welsh politics. When Llywelyn Fawr (Llywelyn the Great) of Gwynedd decided to assemble Welsh lords and princes together so as to swear their allegiance to his son Dafydd, it was to

Ystrad Fflur that he called them in 1238. It is said that within the cemetery many of these princes, and also princes from later ages, are buried. The abbey has, for this reason, been called the Welsh Westminster. It fared badly during the time of Owain Glyndŵr. In 1401 the army of Henry IV was being harried by Glyndŵr's guerrilla fighters and a baggage train belonging to his young son, Henry, was also attacked and robbed. King Henry was furious and marched on Ystrad Fflur determined to vent his anger on this symbol of Welshness. The abbey was plundered; its holy vessels stolen, its buildings looted, and many monks were murdered. Henry ordered that his knights' horses should be tethered at the high altar, with inevitable consequences for the church. His knights drank the abbey's wine cellars dry in a two-day drunken spree, then smashed down the buildings and fired the ruins. In later life Henry is said to have been in an agony of conscience over the acts, though this must have been much later as his son quartered an army here in 1407 during the siege of Aberystwyth castle.

The holiness of the spot meant that, when peace returned, the abbey was rebuilt, and was in constant occupation up until the time of its dissolution. Despite the ravages suffered by the abbey in the early 15th century and an earlier fire following a lightning strike, there is a considerable amount of Norman work in the abbey, including a superb Norman doorway. Not much else of the structure remains intact. Following dissolution the abbeys were customarily stripped of the lead from their roofs and over a period of time the walls collapsed, a decay assisted by locals who used the buildings as a convenient quarry. As a consequence little remains that is immediately discernible to the

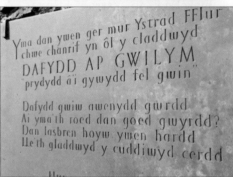

Yma dan ywen ger mur Ystrad FFlur
chwe chanrif yn ôl y claddwyd
DAFYDD AP GWILYM
"prydydd a'i gywydd fel gwin"

Dafydd gwiw awenydd gwrdd
Ai yma'th roed dan goed gwyrdd?
Dan lasbren hoyw ywen hardd
Lle'th gladdwyd y cuddiwyd cerdd
Llu...

layman. Nevertheless the site still has a quiet dignity.

[3] As a contrast to the abbey's cemetery, resting place of many of the medieval princes of Wales, the cemetery of the church beside it holds the remains of **Dafydd ap Gwilym** one of the greatest medieval poets of Europe. Traditionally Dafydd (who died in the late 14th century) was buried under the yew tree, though the memorials to him are very recent. Dafydd was born at Penrhyncoch near Aberystwyth and is renowned for his prose poems on all subjects from love to humour. He is especially fine at describing the natural world.

Walk Directions: [–] denotes Point of Interest
1. From the lay-by at the southern edge of Pontrhydfendigaid [1], continue south along the road towards Tregaron, going gently uphill and soon

reaching a wooden footpath sign on the left.

2. Go through a small wooden gate on the right side of the footpath sign and follow the green track beyond towards the caravans. Go on to the caravan site road and bear left, between the vans. As the road bears right, bear left past the last caravan to reach a stile in the corner.

3. Cross and follow the fence on the left, going through a gate to reach a ruin hidden in the woods, off to the left. There, bear right, going through a gate opening and maintaining direction uphill to reach a stile in the fence at the top of the field. The stile is to the right of the woodland edge beyond. Cross and follow the fence on the left to another stile. Cross and go diagonally right across a field to reach a gate in the top right corner. Go through and turn left immediately through another gate. Now go diagonally right towards a barn.

4. Go through the gate beside the barn and along the farm lane opposite. Beyond the first farm (Gilfachydwn Fawr) the lane degenerates to a tractor track, but remains obvious. When the path forks, go right through a metal gate. Continue ahead to another fork and take the right track again. Go through a gate and follow the now rugged track uphill to a second farm (Gilfachydwn Fach). Go through a gate here and straight ahead along the farm lane to reach a road. There is a fine view from here of the high moorland of the mid-Wales plateau.

5. Turn left. When the road ends, go through a gate

and follow the farm lane beyond. As you approach the farm, a second lane comes in from the left: take this, following it uphill. As it approaches a barn, go through a gate on the left and turn right along the fence (negotiating a curious piece of fencing) to reach a gate into the forest.

6.   Follow the clear bridleway through the forest to reach a forestry road. Maintain direction along this for 50 metres but, as it goes sharp right, bear left along another bridleway between the trees. Follow the bridleway through increasingly excellent woodland to reach a crossing track. Bear left – there is a waymarker here (a blue arrow on a white circle, the waymarker for the unofficial Cambrian Way long-distance footpath).

7.   Walk out of the forest to a stile and continue ahead on a path tunnelled by trees. Shortly, a waymarked post on your left will direct you downhill. Cross the field diagonally to a white post. The ruin on your left is Talwrn. Cross a small stream and a stile then turn right. Follow the left side of the fence to a metal gate with the "Strata Florida #2" waymark on it.

8.   Go through the gate and follow the grassy trail into the woods. When you reach a sign post, continue downhill. Pass a small stream and continue downhill a little further to Nant Glasffrwd where you will cross a footbridge. Go through a gate and continue on the trail with the stream on your left and farm buildings on your right.

9.   A not always obvious path now follows the stream downhill, crossing it once, to reach a footbridge. Cross and follow the stream bank to a gate. Turn left along the road beyond. The Ystrad Fflur car park is to the left, the ruins [2] and church [3] to the right.

10. As the road turns sharp left, go right past the

telephone box and, soon, over a waymarked stile on the left. Cross a footbridge then bear left to the top left corner of the field to a stile. The path now follows Afon Teifi – to your left – all the way back to

Pontrhydfendigaid, with occasional waymarker posts to point the way and a series of stiles and gates to cross. The bank of the river has some lovely trees, mainly hazel and oak. During the early section of this part of the walk, the ruins of an old lead mine can be seen off to the right.

11. When you reach a farm lane, bear left along it to reach the village road. Turn left, crossing the humpbacked bridge over Afon Teifi and passing the road, on the left, for Ystrad Fflur, to return to the start.

Refreshments
There is an inn and a cafe in Pontrhydfendigaid.

Originally published in
Ceredigion Walks

by Richard Sale

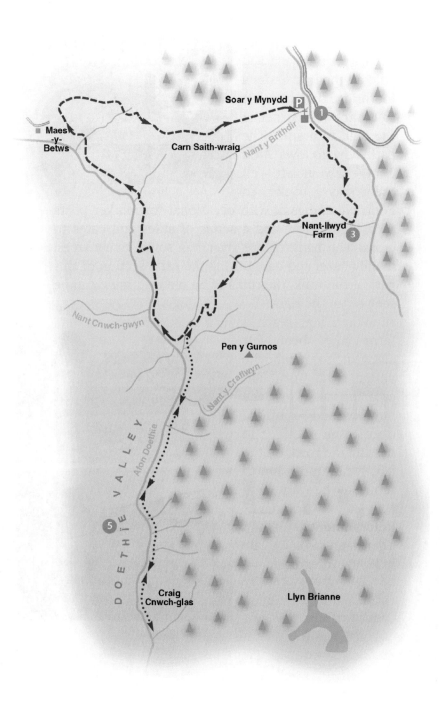

Walk 12
Soar-y-Mynydd

Walk details

Approx distance: *5½ miles/8.8 kilometres or 10 miles/16 kilometres*

Approx time: *4 hours (4½ – 5 hours including the walk to Craig Cnwch-glas)*

O.S. Maps: *1:50 000 Landranger Sheets 146 or 147*
1:25 000 Explorer OL 187 or 200

Start: *Soar-y-Mynydd chapel.*
Grid Ref. SN 784 533

Access: *The chapel lies beside a minor road which reaches the north tip of Llyn Brianne where it forks for Abergwesyn (to the east) and Rhandir-mwyn (to the south). To the north-west this minor road crosses remote country to reach Tregaron. There is no public transport to this chapel.*

Parking: *There is ample parking at the chapel.*

Going: *Difficult. Though the paths are reasonable, this is rugged, remote country.*

Points of Interest:

[1] Farming on the mid-Wales plateau, the land of Elenydd, has always been a lonely occupation. In 1740 the Rev. Howell Harris held a service in Rhiwalog Farm, near Soar-y-Mynydd, the local farmers and their families riding to it on horseback. The services were popular, not only because they allowed the farming families to worship their God in their own language,

but because they were a social occasion, a chance to meet and talk with neighbours. After Harris's death the tradition was maintained, the preachers including William Williams Pantycelyn, the famous Llanymddyfri-born hymn writer. The tradition lasted 80 years. Then, in 1822, the Rev. Ebenezer Richard

vicar of Tregaron and father of Henry Richard, the Apostle of Peace, built **Soar-y-Mynydd chapel** on land donated by John Jones of Nantllwyd Farm. It is still claimed to be the most remote chapel in Wales.

After its construction it was the custom for local farmers to offer hospitality to the preachers, fetching them on horseback from Tregaron or Llanddewibrefi on Saturday and giving them a meal, bed and breakfast. By 1960 congregations had dropped to just 10, but the chapel then saw something of a revival. It is now considered an honour to take the service and congregations have doubled. On the last Sunday in August, a special service often attracts over 50 car-loads of visitors. Inside the chapel the oak chair in the pulpit is a memorial to John Hughes Williams, murdered in 1983, who was instrumental in keeping Soar open when congregations dwindled in the 1960s. Church services are conducted in Welsh between the months of May and October at 2 o'clock in the afternoon.

[2] This walk follows a section of the **Cambrian Way**, a proposed long-distance footpath across the mountainous backbone of Wales, linking Cardiff

and Conwy. The Way
was to have been an
official National Trail,
but the Countryside
Commission, which had
the task of creating the
route, was unable to
tread the tortuous path
between the various
pro- and anti- factions
and, eventually, the
idea was abandoned.
Drawing on the research

of the Commission's field officers the author of this
guide has produced another to an 'unofficial'
Cambrian Way, which uses rights of way to link Cardiff
and Conwy, maintaining the spirit (and almost the
exact line) of the proposed route. See *The Cambrian
Way* by Richard Sale, published by Gwasg Carreg
Gwalch.

[3] Around **Nant-llwyd** there was once a thriving
community, the remains of over 25 squatters' farms
having been discovered. Such farms were built to take
advantage of a 15th century law that gave a man the
right to a parcel of land if, starting at dusk, he could
raise four walls and a chimney and have a fire burning
by the dawn of the next day.

[4] The walk crosses a section of the high mid-Wales
plateau, an area which Giraldus Cambrensis (Gerald of
Wales) called **Elenydd**. Gerald was Archdeacon of
Brecon in the late 12th century and undertook his
famous journey as companion to Baldwin, Archbishop
of Canterbury, who was seeking support, in 1188, for
the Third Crusade. Gerald used the name to describe

the whole of the mountain area of south Wales, as opposed to Eryri, the mountains of North Wales. However, since Giraldus recognised the individual mountain blocks of the Cambrian Mountains what he probably meant by Elenydd was that area between Pumlumon and Mynydd Du. It is likely that the name derives from Afon Elan to the north of the area.

[5] The **Doethïe valley** is one of the finest in mid-Wales, a tight rugged valley, its sides studded with rocky outcrops and wind-bent trees. Near the point where Afon Doethïe joins Afon Tywi the country is a haven for wildlife, there being an RSPB reserve (Dinas)  and a National Nature Reserve. The local area played a crucial role in re-establishing the red kite. Once the red kite was common all over Britain, even being recorded in medieval London scavenging among the rubbish that was the norm in conurbations of that time. But better hygiene in cities and gamekeepers in the country (who saw the birds as a threat to young grouse and pheasants) led to a catastrophic decline in numbers. By the end of the 19th century the red kite had been made extinct in England and Scotland and was also declining in Wales. By the 1960s a mere handful of pairs (perhaps as few as six) clung on in the wilderness of mid-Wales. The kite is largely a carrion feeder, though it will take live rabbits and rodents. It takes young birds, too, but these are more likely to be gulls or crows: the red kite was never the threat to game

birds that the gamekeepers feared. It also needs trees in which to perch and nest. The country near the Doethïe valley was ideal and it was here that the main effort was made to halt the decline in numbers and then to promote an increase. This has been remarkably successful. By 1989 the RSPB/Nature Conservation Council were able to release red kites into England – they used birds from Spain and Sweden rather than Wales, but the Welsh population was by then showing a healthy population rise. Birds have now also been released in Scotland. In 1998 there were over 150 breeding pairs of kites in Wales, as well as about 75 pairs in England and 20 in Scotland.

The red kite is a magnificent bird, a rich chestnut-brown in colour and with a deeply forked tail. Walkers in the Doethïe valley are very likely to see one: its appearance, working the updrafts from the steep valley sides, is likely to be the highlight of the day.

[6] This track is part of an **old drovers' road** from Llanddewi Brefi, continuing eastwards beyond Soar chapel towards the border with England. In the days before refrigeration, cattle, pigs and sheep, and even chickens, turkeys and geese, were brought to market live, drovers escorting the animals along defined drove-roads. A big drove must have been a magnificent sight and the drovers certainly earned their pay – imagine having to keep flocks of fowls on the move as well as the herds. It is said that the birds had their feet dipped in pitch to harden them for the march and that cattle were shod to ease the load on their feet. The blacksmiths who shoed the cattle were said to be both highly skilled and extremely brave, both of which seem to be indisputable.

Inns were set up along the roads for the use of the

drovers, who were rich on their return journeys and, therefore, very popular with landlords. The rich drovers were also popular with highwaymen who lay in wait on quieter sections of the roads. It was to try to combat the highwaymen and to reduce the losses of heavy drinking that banks such as Tregaron's Black Sheep Bank were established.

Twm Siôn Cati

One famous drover was Twm Siôn Cati. He was the illegitimate son of Catherine Jones of Tregaron, who named him Thomas Jones. Because of his lack of a legitimate father, he became known as Twm Siôn Cati. He was a man of some renown, and referred to by poets, during his own lifetime. Born about 1530, he married a Brecon widow late in life and was a justice of peace for the old shires of Brecon and Carmarthen and Major of Brecon. His will, dated 17 May 1609, still exists – he left nine head of cattle to an illegitimate son and everything else to his widow Johan (Joan) – but the legends surrounding him, which transform him into a Welsh Robin Hood type of figure, but one with rather more humour and a great deal less tragedy than the original, are largely the work of Llewelyn Pritchard, an early 19th century writer. One story of Twm, related by a local to George Borrow and recounted in his book *Wild Wales*, tells of Twm stealing a bull with a short tail and attaching a longer tail to the short one before taking it to market to sell. There the original owner recognises the bull, but is surprised by the long tail. He claims the tail must be false, so Twm takes a knife and cuts it off, taking care to cut the real tail above the false one. The bull roars, blood flows and the farmer, convinced he has made a mistake, apologises to Twm.

But Twm now insists the farmer buy the bull, claiming he only mutilated it at his request. The people who had gathered to watch the incident side with Twm and the farmer is forced to buy his own stolen bull at a high price.

Twm's reputed hideout during his 'loveable rogue' period was on the RSPB's Dinas reserve, at Grid Ref. SN 786 466.

Walk Directions: **[–] denotes Point of Interest**
1. From the chapel [1] follow the obvious path [2] heading south-eastwards (over the cattle grid, along the track signed 'Locked Gate Ahead') bearing right when this forks. The track now continues straightforwardly to Nantllwyd Farm [3].
2. With the farmhouse on your right, find the waymark on a farm building directing you to go right between the buildings and the farmhouse. Walk up the slight gradient to the gates, continuing along the clear moorland path [4]. When the path becomes unclear bear southwards crossing the field between two hills (Grid Ref. SN 776 519). Walk towards a metal kissing gate and follow the trail descending to the valley floor. There are some great views of the Doethïe valley from this point [5]. Descend gently and cross a couple of streams which drain the plateau. Beyond the second stream the path crosses a broad ridge, and then descends steeply to reach a path fork close to the Nant Lluest Fach.

3. The right-hand path

here is the return route. For the moment, bear left and follow the clear path through woodland to reach Afon Doethïe. Now follow the river southwards [5]. This is an out – and – back detour and can be of any length: to savour this magnificent valley it should be walked at least as far as Craig Cnwch-glas (on the valley's eastern side, at Grid Reference SN 766 494). The views of Doethïe valley's rugged landscape are fantastic in all weather conditions and are worth the extra 2.67 kilometres (1.6 miles).

4.   After the detour along the Doethïe valley, return to the path fork near Nant Lluest Fach and take the other branch. The trail does become non-existent at times but keep to a north-westerly direction and the trail will become clear again. The trail also drops to Afon Doethïe, but follows the river northwards through exquisite country to reach, after about 3.5 kilometres – just over 2 miles – a crossing track. To the left the track goes to the remote Youth Hostel of Ty'n-y-cornel. To the right it can be followed [6] all the way to Capel Soar along the trail passing Carn Saith Wraig on your right.

Refreshments
None. Walkers must bring their own or drive to Llanddewi Brefi, Tregaron, Rhandir-mwyn or Abergwesyn.

The nearest petrol station is in Lampeter and Llanymddyfri.

Originally published in
Ceredigion Walks

by Richard Sale

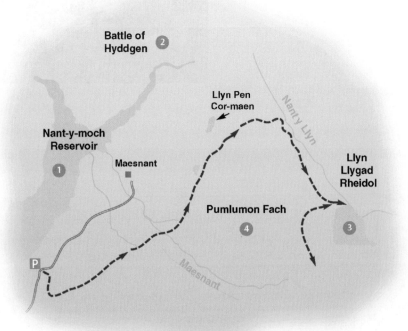

Walk 13

Llyn Llygad Rheidol – Pumlumon Fach

Walk details

Approx distance: *5 miles/8 kilometres*

Approx time:	*From the starting point to Llyn Llygad Rheidol Reservoir it takes approximately an hour. From the reservoir the ascent to Pumlumon Fach is poorly defined and steep therefore it may take between 1½ – 2 hours.*
O.S. Maps:	*1:50 000 Landranger Sheet 135* *1:25 000 Explorer OL 213*
Start:	*Junction of minor road with track at Grid Reference SN 768 874.*
Access:	*From the A44 just east of Ponterwyd, take the country lane at Grid Reference 751 812, signposted for the Nant-y-moch dam. However, before reaching the dam, take the right turn at Grid Reference 763 864 to the start point. From the A487, follow signs for Nant-y-moch dam at Talybont. The narrow country road winds through farmland and leads to the reservoir.*
Parking:	*There should be room to park one or two cars off the road near the start point.*
Going:	*Strenuous – involves about 325m ascent in total. Tracks and open country. Walking boots are essential.*
Please note:	*The track to Llyn Llygad Rheidol reservoir is unsuitable for vehicles as the track is very rocky with several pools of water. Take care when walking past the pools on the track as there may be steep*

> *drops. Also, the weather is unpredicatable at most times. Mist and fog is common at Pumlumon therefore take care when attempting to ascend the mountains. When weather is unclear do not attempt to walk up the mountain as there is no clear track.*

A fine mountain walk, including a trip to the summit of Pumlumon Fawr's little brother, plus a glimpse of several unexpected mountain tarns. The final haul up to the summit of Pumlumon Fach is not long, but quite steep. This route may be treated as an alternative way up to Pumlumon Fawr, as the walk from Pumlumon Fach to Pumlumon Fawr is fairly straightforward.

Points of Interest:
[1] Nant-y-moch Reservoir
This reservoir, built between 1957 and 1960 and officially opened in 1964, takes water from a number of rivers, including the Hyddgen and Hengwm, which effectively feed the infant Rheidol which has its source at Llyn Llygad Rheidol (see below). Its function is to provide the water to power the Rheidol Hydro-Electric Scheme. The out flowing waters beyond the dam at Grid Reference SN 753 860 (easily visited by car) form the Rheidol proper.
[2] Site of the **Battle of Hyddgen**, 1401. By the beginning of the fifteenth century, the Welsh rebellion against the English crown, led by Owain Glyndŵr, was in full swing. Attempts by the English King, Henry IV,

to crush the rebellion were failing in the face of Welsh guerrilla tactics. For the most part, the outnumbered Welsh avoided pitched battles, but in 1401, in the Hyddgen Valley in Pumlumon, a force lead by Owain Glyndŵr were set upon by an army of English and Flemish soldiers some 1500 strong (many of whom were from the Landsker of South Pembrokeshire, and who were set firmly against Owain's goal of a Welsh state independent of England), and a ferocious battle ensued. Heavily outnumbered, Owain's men were surrounded, and were left with no alternative but to fight their way out. The outcome was one of Glyndŵr's most spectacular victories, for the King's men were utterly routed, and before long Glyndŵr would be in control of virtually all of Wales (see below). The site of the battle is commemorated now by a standing stone, which may just about be visible in the Hyddgen valley from this point.

Owain Glyndŵr

It is difficult to overstate the importance of Owain ap Gruffudd, otherwise known as Owain Glyndŵr, in Welsh history. He is the national hero of heroes, the ultimate symbol of Welsh nationhood, and his significance, perhaps, lies primarily in the sphere of symbolism rather than of his historically verifiable exploits.

He was an unlikely hero. Born into a wealthy Marcher family, he was descended both from Prince Llywelyn and from the ruling family of Deheubarth in South Wales. Yet his early life was unremarkable, and it is something of an irony that he spent much of his life fighting for the English cause in a distinguished, though not particularly spectacular, military career. By the time he reached middle age, Owain was living the life of a retired country gentleman, owning considerable lands around the Dee. At this time, Wales was fully in the control of the English crown. There were gripes, of course, particularly in rural Wales, where the English domination was resented. However, the English King, Richard II, was relatively popular, and there was little outward sign of the rebellion that was to follow.

It was political machinations in England that were to fan the flames of war. Towards the end of the fourteenth century, Richard II was ousted by Henry Bolingbroke, who took the crown to become Henry IV. The new King was far from popular, however, and many of his actions outraged the Welsh, though it was an obscure dispute over land that sparked rebellion. One of the King's henchmen, Lord Grey of Ruthin, unlawfully seized some land in the north east of Wales, and he was backed up in his claim by the King. The former owner of the land was not at all happy about this – this landowner was Owain Glyndŵr.

It is not at all clear at this point what Owain's motivations were. Some said he was being manipulated by the Tudor family, who were later to seize the English throne after the Wars of the Roses. Others said he was working to secure the return to the throne of the ousted Richard II. Nevertheless, by now Owain had abandoned all pretence of loyalty to the despised Henry IV and he set about gathering an army to oppose the King, claiming for himself the title of Prince of Wales. Welsh outrage at the actions of Henry IV were quite sufficient to ensure that Owain enjoyed massive popular support, and Welshmen from all over the country – and from the Welsh diaspora in London and Oxford – flocked to his side.

By 1400, the Welsh were in full rebellion, and marched on several English castles. Henry, of course, had to respond, though Owain's men remained elusive. For most of the rebellion, outright pitched battles were avoided by the Welsh, and guerrilla tactics were the order of the day. For a long time, these tactics were startlingly effective, and by 1406 Owain was in control of virtually the whole of Wales. So successful was Owain that even his enemies started to believe that he was more than human; many believed that he was able to control the weather, as several of Henry's forays into Wales were thwarted not by Welsh military action but by ferocious rainstorms. He established a parliament at Machynlleth, and for the last time in history Wales was effectively a free and independent nation.

It could not last. If nothing else would, then sheer superiority of numbers on the part of the English would prevail, and the small nation of Wales would be slowly ground down and exhausted by an unsustainable effort against superior force. In 1409, Owain lost virtually his entire family when Harlech Castle fell to Henry, and the war was soon won decisively by the

English. In 1412, Owain was offered a free pardon by the King, but he refused to take it, and remained a fugitive. It was almost certainly this action that ensured Owain's unique place in history and mythology, for no-one knows what really happened to him after this. It is thought that he died in 1416, at the house of a relative in Herefordshire, but this is uncertain. It was not the destiny of Owain to die and be mourned by his people. Rather, it was his destiny to vanish mysteriously from the historical stage, still clinging to the rightness of his cause, and to become an enduring legend and symbol of Welsh nationhood.

Only King Arthur – who may not have been Welsh at all – is enveloped in more myth and folklore than Owain Glyndŵr. Indeed, perhaps Owain became a latter day King Arthur, and while Owain has no grave that can identified he can be said, by the storytellers and patriots, to be merely sleeping, deep in some Welsh mountain, waiting for the day that he can return and lead Wales, once more, from the domination of England and into its rightful place in the community of nations.

[3] **Llyn Llygad Rheidol** This mountain lake-cum-reservoir, which forms the effective source of the Rheidol (although it may be argued that one of the

many streams feeding the lake may be regarded as the true source), is tucked away beneath the crags of Graig Las to the east and Pumlumon Fawr to the south, and it is perhaps the one failing of

Pumlumon Fawr itself that you cannot get a really good view of Llyn Llygad Rheidol from the summit. However, the lake is easily visible from the initial climb up to Pumlumon Fach, although once again the summit does not allow good views to be had in safety, as the north eastern side of Pumlumon Fach drops almost vertically down to the banks of the lake. In fact, the lake lies within a fabulous natural amphitheatre, enclosed on three sides by Pen Cerrig Tewion, Pumlumon Fawr and Pumlumon Fach. There is a pumping station at the north side of the lake. Note that although it might be tempting for the adventurous to nip across Nant y Llyn to make an assault on Pen Cerrig Tewion (which is slightly higher than Pumlumon Fach, though an easier and less steep climb), this is likely to be dangerous. The nant is just wide enough to make stepping stones necessary, and the only candidates with easy striking distance of Llyn Llygad Rheidol are distinctly dodgy. Be warned!

[4] **Pumlumon Fach** I have noted elsewhere that one tends to feel rather sorry for Pumlumon Fach, doomed to spend eternity in the shadow of Pumlumon Fawr, but it has its own charms. Just east of north you can see the twin cairns of Banc Llechwedd-mawr, while to the north east Pen Cerrig Tewion stands imperiously, just nine metres higher but seemingly determined to make every centimetre count. To the south east, of course, stands Pumlumon Fawr, while the lesser hump of Pumlumon Fach stands

to the east (a detour to this on your way down is fairly straightforward). You may just about be able to see the south side of Nant-y-moch Reservoir poking its head out away to the south west. The summit of Pumlumon Fach, which is dotted with pieces of white quartz, is distinctly bleaker than that of Pumlumon Fawr, having none of the wire fences, large cairns or shelters that adorn the latter. While this gives Pumlumon Fach much more of a feel of isolation and wilderness than its big brother, it also means that the shelter available on the summit of Pumlumon Fawr is not available here. The summit of Pumlumon Fach is not a place to be stranded.

Walk Directions: [–] **denotes Point of Interest**
1.   From the start point in the shadow of Drosgol on the banks on the Nant-y-moch Reservoir [1], follow the obvious track initially south, then north east, around the disused quarries at Bryn y Beddau. The path heads off uphill quite steeply for a while and then it levels out between the unnamed nant north east of Bryn y

Beddau and Maesnant. Continue on past the three tarns west of Fainc Ddu.

2.   At this point in the walk, you get perhaps the very best views of the Hyddgen Valley away to the north, and you can see from here the site of the Battle of Hyddgen, 1401, down in the valley [2]. After passing Llyn Pen-cor-maen, the track bends round to the east, then heads off south east, shadowing Nant y

Llyn to Llyn Llygad Rheidol [3].

3. From Llyn Llygad Rheidol, it becomes necessary to make the tortuous ascent of Pumlumon Fach. There is a paucity of decent paths here, and it is necessary more or less to freelance uphill, somewhere between south and south west. The easiest way uphill is pretty obvious – not least because most of the alternatives look

nigh on impossible – and you may be able to make out a very poorly defined path marking the best route (from the point where the track bends to the left at Grid Reference SN 790 879), though it is very steep in parts and care must be taken, especially in less than ideal weather. Following this way up, you will emerge between the two humps of Pumlumon Fach: on the right lies the lower of the two humps (at about 660m above sea level), but the true summit (at 668 metres) lies atop the hump to your left. Head straight uphill to your left, and you will soon emerge (probably rather breathless) at the summit [4], which is marked by a rather sorry-looking cairn.

4. Pick your way back down to the track leading to Llyn Llygad Rheidol. There are some excellent spots on the way down to eat your sandwiches in comfort – the prevailing winds should be at your back at this

point, and the crags provide natural shelter and convenient seats. After regaining the track, it is now a simple matter of re-tracing your steps to the start point, following the track all the way.

Facilities:

There are few facilities in the vicinity. The nearest place to find a shop or a pub is Ponterwyd on the A44. However, Llangurig (about a dozen miles east along the A44) is well provided with tea rooms and bed and breakfast facilities. Devil's Bridge (about 3 miles south west along the A44 and A4120) also has numerous facilities. The Nant yr Arian Forest Centre near Ponterwyd is designated as a Kite Country Centre. The road that is north-east of the Nant-y-moch Reservoir leads to Talybont (17 miles from where the car is parked by the start of the walk) where there are toilet facilities, petrol station and the Llew Du Hotel and Restaurant.

Safety Notes:

The final ascent to the summit of Pumlumon Fach on this walk is pretty steep, and walkers would be well advised to make the ascent only in decent weather. Having said that, the well defined track from the start point to Llyn Llygad Rheidol provides few navigational difficulties, and the only problem you are likely to have in this respect is if you get stuck in mist on or near the top of Pumlumon Fach, in which case you are faced with two choices. First, you can re-trace your steps roughly just east of north to the main track, but take great care among the crags. Particularly, take extreme care that you do not wander off route and end up heading for the almost vertical drop to the north down towards Llyn Llygad Rheidol. Although the descent down the craggy path to Llyn Llygad Rheidol can be tricky at the best of times, it would be preferable to take this route down – very slowly and very carefully – since the alternative is likely to be inconvenient in the extreme. The alternative route is to head south south east to the summit of Pumlumon Fawr, and follow one of the safety routes off there to Eisteddfa-Gurig. This will avoid the worst of the steep crags, but it will take you a long distance out of your way, and you will probably need to summon help to get back to your car on reaching Eisteddfa-Gurig.

Originally published in
Circular Walks in Central Wales

by Stephen Edwards

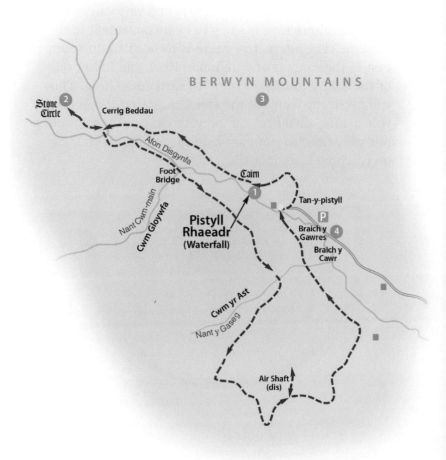

Walk 14
Stone circle at Rhos y Beddau from Pistyll Rhaeadr

Walk details

Approx distance: *4 miles/6½ kilometres*

Approx time: *2½ – 3 hours*

O.S. Maps: *1:50 000 Landranger 125*
                1:25 000 Explorer OL 255

Start: *Tan-y-Pistyll*

Access: *From the centre of Llanrhaeadr-ym-Mochnant,*
                follow the minor single-track road north-west
                (signed Waterfall Rhaeadr) on the north side of
                Afon Rhaeadr to the end – approximately 4 miles
                (6 kilometres).

Parking: *There are 2 small, free parking areas on the left*
                hand side, about 100 metres from the end of the
                road; or there is a pay car park (modest charge) at
                the end of the road. Grid Ref. SJ 074 295

Height Gain: *About 250 metres.*

Going: *Easy, but with a vigorous start.*

Facilities: *There are toilets, a telephone and a small café at the*
                beginning of the walk. The latter is not always open
                in the winter. There is also a small family campsite
                with limited facilities.

Overview: *A circular walk, starting at an impressive waterfall,*
                passing a stone circle and returning via a disused
                lead mine.

This walk could be used as a basis for reaching the remote Nuttall, Post Gwyn, when the grade would become moderate; or even the main Berwyn summits (Cadair Bronwen, Cadair Berwyn and Moel Sych), when the grade would become strenuous.

Points of Interest:

[1] **Pistyll Rhaeadr** Although there are excellent views down the valley, it is not easy to get a good view of the

falls from this side. In fact, the best view of the falls is probably gained from the terrace outside the café at the base of the falls, where you can enjoy the view and share your scones with the chaffinches. If there is not too much water in the river, you can cross it just above the falls and take a cautious view of the water charging over the top of the fall. In geological terms these falls are very young, only having been formed during the last ice age.

[2] **Stone Circle** This stone circle is made up of small stones and it is hard to find amongst the ferns and bracken in summer and autumn. It is about thirteen metres in diameter and an unusual feature, at least for Welsh sites, is a 50 metre avenue comprising of two rows of stones, running east to west which aim tangentially to the south side of the circle. These stones may not actually be related to the stone circle at all. There is a faint depression in the centre of the circle, which may be the remains of a burial cyst.

[3] **Berwyn Mountains** The views of the valley from here below and arguably the most scenic in the

Berwyn, especially if you walk 50 metres to your left onto a promontory high above the valley. From here, you get a good long range view of the falls, plus a view of the main Berwyn summits to the north.

[4] Almost 200 metres below on the valley floor towards the base of the falls, you can see two large pinnacles – **Braich y Gawres and Braich y Cawr** – which look most out of place in the green meadows. They are the result of glacial activity during the last ice age.

[5] **Disused Lead Mine** The leat, which carried water from the falls, was used for the lead mining operations. Lead was mined here from Roman times until the end of the last century. Despite not being used for a hundred years, the hillside has still not recovered and is littered with spoil material. Should you feel inclined to investigate the workings you will almost certainly be disappointed. It is a very steep climb with 100 metres or more of ascent, and reveals nothing more than spoil from the mine. At the bottom of the incline there are a few more remains of the mining operation, and the wall of the leat is clearly visible.

Walk Directions:

[-] **denotes point of interest**

1. Take the way marked 'path' just before the toilets in the pay car park. The path goes up through the trees, and you then turn left up a very steep zigzag hill. At the top of the steep climb, leave the main path and go down the gentle slope to your left through the woods, to reach the top of the falls [1].

2. Follow the north bank of this small river (Afon Disgynfa) through the woods, which is often boggy. Cross a stile and re-join the original track shortly after leaving the woods. Now the walk continues up the gently sloping valley. When the trail forks, bear right

then bear left at the next fork which is shortly afterwards. The trail becomes untraceable which is densely covered with fern. Continue to maintain a westerly direction following the course of the river.

3. After about a 1.5 kilometres, you reach a substantial ruined sheep fold where a stream, Nant y Cerrigduon, joins the river from the north. Cross this stream and, taking the right of the two tracks up a steep slope, you will arrive at the stone circle after about 250 metres [2].

Alternative Longer Routes: From this point you could head south west across the valley and climb the remote Nuttall, Post Gwyn. From the summit, you go in a south-easterly direction, rejoining the shorter route at Craig-y-Mwn. It is also possible to ascend Moel Sych via its western spur, but this is not as pleasant as the other routes to this summit.

4. You now retrace your steps for about 500 metres and after passing through a fence, you follow it down the slope to your right until you meet the river. This is crossed wherever possible, dependent upon how much rain there has been recently. On the far bank, just over one hundred metres from the fence, you look for a wooden footbridge and a path going south-east which starts where a stream (Nant Cwm-main) joins the river from the south. However, this path, like many in the Berwyn, although easily found on the OS map is faint and, certainly for the next few hundred metres, hard to

find. You aim for a stile at a fenced corner on the right-hand side of a few conifer trees. Continue along the trail through a field which eventually becomes more defined and the crags of Craig-y-Mwn come into view [3]. These are the only real cliffs in the Berwyn, and not at all typical of the area. You continue uphill to the top of the crags and shortly after you cross a stream (Nant y Gaseg) that plunges over the cliffs. Continue walking along the wide track.

5. You can now follow a faint precipitous path to your right (south-east) which cuts across the face of the slope, running steeply down to the valley floor. The path is exposed. Alternatively you can avoid that path by staying on top of the crags for a few hundred metres, before turning left onto the main track back to the valley. After about 300 metres you reach the incline running down from the old lead mine, and if you follow the incline a further 50 metres downhill, you join the main path going back to Pistyll Rhaeadr alongside an old leat [5].

6. From the bottom of the incline you follow the path alongside the leat north-west back towards the falls.

After 300 metres you join a wood and walk along the edge, where you see the two very strange rock pinnacles – Braich y Gawres and Braich y Cawr [4] – in the fields on your
right. There is now a choice of routes. Either follow way-marked paths across the fields, which bring you to the road near to the car park; or more scenically, continue along the course of the leat to the
falls, where there is a small bridge crossing the river directly below the falls near to the café.

Originally published in
Walks in and around the Berwyn Mountains

by John Tranter

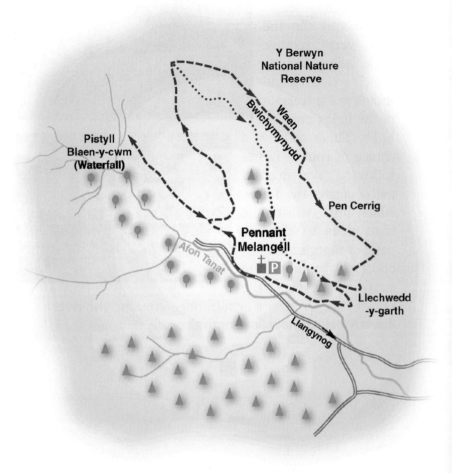

Walk 15

Cwm Pennant Melangell – Santes Melangell's Church

Walk details

Approx distance: *5 miles/7.7 kilometres*

Approx time: 4 hours

O.S. Maps: *1:50 000 Landranger 125*
1:25 000 Explorer OL 255 or Explorer OL 239

Start and Finish: *Pennant Melangell church*

Access: *Pennant Melangell is reached by following a narrow road westerly for approximately two miles (three kilometres) from Llangynog.*

Parking: *There is a small car park next to the church. Grid Ref. SJ 024 265*

Height Gain: *About 400 metres.*

Going: *Moderate, with a short pathless section.*

Facilities: *None other than a small gift shop in the church.*

Overview: *This circular walk climbs out of the valley past an attractive waterfall, and up onto the Berwyn plateau.*

This walk starts at a truly magical place in beautiful surroundings. Santes Melangell's church is about 800 years old, and contains a shrine to Santes Melangell. This shrine, reconstructed in 1991, is the oldest known in northern Europe, and is visited by thousands of pilgrims each year.

At the end of the church, there is a reconstruction on 12th century foundations, containing what is thought to be the 8th century grave slab of Santes Melangell. The church contains many other gems. In the church yard there are several beautiful yew trees of great age – possibly 2000 years old. Although very few people live in the area today, the site has been occupied for many centuries, and the church is built on a Bronze Age settlement. Just to visit this church, which is open daily and has a small gift shop, is worth the journey. A few years ago it was in serious disrepair, but has recently been restored. The restoration is excellent and the building has a timbered belfry, typical of an area with poor stone.

Walk Directions:

1.   From the car park, continue north-west along the lane. You will pass the St. Melangell Centre on your right and will soon see a sign on your right directing to the waterfall. Go through the wooden gate and keep to the right side of the field. Walk ahead to a way-marked gate and head uphill north-westwards to another wooden gate in the corner of the field. Bear slightly left (west) to a trail which leads to the waterfall, Pistyll Blaen-y-cwm, in about 1.1 kilometres. This track,

obviously of great age, begins to fade and is virtually non-existent by the time you reach the falls.

The waterfalls, again unsung gems of the Berwyn, are very attractive, falling very quickly through 100 metres in a few large steps. It is a beautiful and peaceful place to take a picnic.

2. Head back to the wooden gate (Grid Ref. SJ 019 270) and footpath signpost which directs you to turn left (north-east) up the hill to another gate on your right. Follow the trail for 230 metres to a field where the path becomes barely visible. There are fantastic views of Cwm Pennant from this point. Bear north up the hill for 360 metres to a wooden gate. As you walk to the gate, keep to the left trail which goes uphill when it forks. Go through the gate and follow the trail to another gate. The

trail has become challenging and steep with thick, marshy grassland. You are now walking an ancient track running north-west near the top of the valley. Head to the plateau which is 500 metres away. When you reach the plateau, the views are spectacular which stretch from the Berwyn Mountains to Snowdonia National Park and beyond. Unspoilt and wild, the landscape is tranquil and the perfect setting for a sanctuary such as Santes Melangell's church. After spending time on the Berwyn plateau (Grid Ref. SJ 019 279) head up north-east onto the moor. The going now

gets tougher as the bilberries are replaced by heather. Cross two fences at convenient gates, and you reach the main east-west boundary fence about 700 metres from the track.

The scenery is now very different from that in the valley. To the north, the heather-clad moor stretches away towards the main bulk of the Berwyn. Moel Sych is prominent, and Post Gwyn is easily found. At 540 metres high, this can be a very desolate place, and you have now seen the full gamut of Berwyn scenery.

Alternative Shorter Walk: If the weather has turned for the worse and you would like to cut the journey short, there is an alternative route which is a mile shorter. After crossing the fences, make your way down the valley ridge. The path appears and disappears along the way but head south towards the forest to find a clear trail. Along the trail you will come across small streams which are crossable. You will soon descend to a gate near the forest, enter it, and continue to walk along a trail where a stone wall will be on your left with a waymarked pole. In a few metres the path forks, keep to the right path and follow it down through a forest to

some building at Llechwedd-y-garth. Turn right to a path that'll lead you back to the car park.

3. Head right (east) along the boundary fence, which follows the ridge. The going

is reasonable, though sometimes boggy. After a kilometre or so, Cwm Rhiwarth comes into view on your left, and you reach Pen Cerrig (495 metres) (Grid Ref. SJ 031 271) after two and a half kilometres.

From here there are good views south-west, down into Cwm Pennant. Moel Dimoel, due south across the valley, is very striking, since it is extraordinarily steep near its summit. To the west is Craig Rhiwarth, which does not look as challenging as when close up.

4.   From Pen Cerrig you descend south-east along the ridge, still pathless, for about 500 metres to a low point. Here you meet a right of way across the ridge, but it is not easy to find and obviously not much used. You turn right, south-west, back down into Cwm Pennant. After about 400 metres you reach a forest and turn right, north-west, contouring across the hillside, and keeping the forest on your left. After 700 metres you reach a sheepfold on the forest edge, and turn left (south) on to a track alongside the forest. The track soon swings south-east and you follow it down through the forest, reaching some buildings at Llechwedd-y-garth after about one kilometre. Turn right through the buildings and after about twenty metres, turn right again to join the 'Pererindod Melangell' trail which heads west to reach the car park at Pennant Melangell in less than a kilometre.

Longer Alternative Walk:

This walk can be started and finished from the car park (Grid Ref. SJ 054 262) in Llangynog. Pennant Melangell is reached by turning left out of the car park and following the minor road (1st right) for just over three kilometres. There are several paths to the right (north) of the road, but these are often hard to find, particularly in the summer when they are overgrown, and it is easy to get lost. Allied to the fact that many of the tracks are marked Private, No Access, it is probably best to stay on the minor road, which fortunately has very little traffic. From Pennant Melangell follow the original route to the low point below Pen Cerrig. Here you turn left, north-east, and cross the fence (no stile). There are only animal tracks here, but suddenly you come to an ancient track heading north, and down into the valley. Although obviously not much used today, it must have seen a lot of traffic at some stage because there is significant erosion. At the far side of a small wood, about 400 metres down the track, you reach a stream. There is a right of way on the near-side of this stream, going north-east down to the road, but it is hard to find. Every now and then you find a stile with a yellow arrow to assure you that you are on the right track. At the road, you turn right and you can follow

this road for about two and a half kilometres back to Llangynog. Alternatively, after 500 metres, pick up the footpath by entering Glanyrafon and crossing the footbridge. Follow it across the valley to join the B4391 near Tanyffordd. Llangynog is about 1200 metres down the road. This adds approximately six kilometres distance, but negligible climbing to the walk.

Originally published in
Walks in and around the Berwyn Mountains

by John Tranter

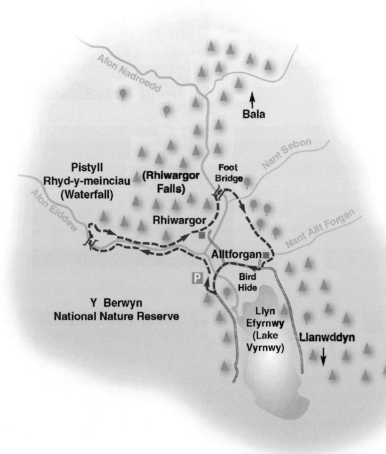

Walk 16

Llyn Efyrnwy (*Lake Vyrnwy*) – two short walks

Walk details

Approx distance: *6 miles/10 kilometres*

Approx time: *Rhiwargor Falls Walk – 1 hour*
Craig Garth-bwlch Trail – 1½ hours

O.S. Maps: *1:50 000 Landranger 125*
1:25 000 Explorer OL 23 and Explorer OL 239

Start: *Walk 1: Rhiwargor car park at the northermost point of the lake. (Grid Ref. SH 964 242)*
Walk 2: the Village car park in Llanwddyn. (Grid Ref. SJ 018 190)

Access: *About 9 miles west of Llanfyllin on the B4398 or about 6 miles south-west of Penybontfawr, on the B4391. May be reached from Bala on very minor roads.*
Bus services are very infrequent to this rural location, with only one bus service from Oswestry to Lake Vyrnwy on a Wednesday afternoon each week.
The nearest railway station is Welshpool, more than 20 miles away. Taxi's are not readily available at the station and must be booked in advance.

Parking: *Rhiwargor car park (Grid Ref. SH 964 242) and the Village car park (Grid Ref. SJ 018 190) for the second walk.*

Height Gain: *Minimal on the first walk; about 100 metres on the second walk*

Going: *Easy, but can be extended to moderate.*

Facilities:	*A visitors notice board and picnic area are located near the Rhiwargor car park. There are a variety of facilities near the Village car park, including a Tourist Information Office, an RSPB shop, Visitor Centre, Craft Shops and a cafe.*
Overview:	*Two easy walks, next to a lake in a beautiful valley, with lots of bird life based on the Rhiwargor, Water and Craig Garth – bwlch trails, which are easily joined by a short car journey. Leaflets for these trails may be obtained at the Tourist Information Office.*

Walk 1: Rhiwargor Falls Walk
(2.3 miles/3.7 kilometres)

1. After sharing your snack with the chaffinches in the picnic area, follow the way-mark path north-west through the picnic area to the river (Afon Eiddew). Stay on the south bank of the river and continue west, with occasional glimpses of the waterfall. For a close view of the waterfall, ignore any way-marks and continue on the south bank. You reach the base of the falls about one kilometre from the car park.

These are some of the most impressive falls in the Berwyn: although not as high as those in Pistyll Rhaeadr, they carry a much greater volume of water (very peaty). They are magnificent at any time, but particularly so after heavy

rain. They fall about one hundred metres in a series of large steps, in a distance of less than two hundred metres.

For a close examination of the falls, you can follow a path on their left hand side, but our route goes back for about 100 metres to a wooden foot bridge on your left (north).

2. Cross the bridge, turn left alongside the felled forest, and you reach the bottom of the falls on the opposite side in a short distance. Those with nimble feet can reach the same place by using the stepping stones from the far side of the falls.

Alternative longer route: You can continue up alongside the falls, and out onto the moors. You need to be prepared to get your feet wet, and it is necessary to cross a couple of fences without the benefit of stiles. You may have to walk quite a long way before you can cross the river, but this is usually possible on an S bend, where there is an island in the middle, with a couple of small jumps or large strides. This is about half a kilometre after you have passed the ruins of Blaen-y-coed on the far bank. You can head north-west from here to the summit of Bwlan (528 metres), but this is not a very exciting hill. However, you get good views to the west and north of the south-western Berwyn summits. For the Berwyn, there is remarkably little heather, and walking is not too tough. Descend south to Blaen-y-coed. The ruins are quite extensive and obviously the area has not been used for a long time, since many of the remains are grass-covered. Follow the path (often very faint) south-east from Blaen-y-coed, high above the falls (on your right) and with excellent views, back to the forest and then descend very steeply to your right (south-west) alongside the forest fence to rejoin the original route just below the falls. This adds about 5 kilometres distance, and 300 metres ascent, to the walk.

3. Having finished looking at the falls, turn around and walk back towards the forest, but now stay on the main track that runs down the left hand side. You disappear into the forest and after about a kilometre the track arrives at the B4393. Turn left and you descend gently in a northerly direction.

4. The track is way-marked with green arrows. After a few hundred metres you meet a rickety bridge on the right which you cross, and again turn right, back down the far side of the river (Afon Nadroedd). You follow the path round and down through the forest, and it takes on the appearance of an ancient track because across the gently sloping hillside, there is a horizontal section about three or four metres wide which, although not well-trodden today, has a row of very ancient trees along its right-hand side. Carefully cross a stream and continue to the next stile which

leads you to field. Cross the field and head for the road.

Cross the road almost immediately, and follow the signs to the RSPB Hide, which is only about 200 metres down this track.

The hide is ideally placed for looking at the birds on the water just in front of you, and there are plenty of illustrations indicating the kind of birds you are likely to see. However, whether you happen to see them or not is quite a matter of chance and the time of year.

Retrace your steps from the hide back to the road, and turn left. After half a kilometre you will arrive back at the car park. This is a good opportunity to eat lunch in the picnic area.

Walk 2: Craig Garth-bwlch Trail
(2.7 miles/4.3 kilometres)

1. To reach the second walk, you have to drive 5 miles down the south side of Lake Vyrnwy. Drive straight past the dam and after about half a kilometre, almost at the end of the road, there are several car parks. The one down a short road on your left (the Village car park) is convenient for the walk. Walk back up to the dam, and turn right to walk along the top of it.

There are several signs giving you information about the dam which was completed in 1891 and flooded the village of Llanwddyn in the process. Looking out across Lake Vyrnwy, which is Severn Trent Water's largest reservoir, you can see to your right the Gothic Tower, where water leaves the reservoir on its way to the inhabitants of Liverpool.

Continue across the dam and turn right at the end of it. Almost immediately, there is a way-marked path

 on your right dropping down below the dam into the valley. The valley is now a wooden sculpture park exhibiting works from Welsh and international artists. In the valley you cross a dry riverbed, where the river was diverted whilst the dam was being built. Continue along the pleasant way-marked path, past a weir on the river, until eventually you come to a footbridge. Once across, turn right and shortly onto a path through the trees alongside the river. You now pass the weir on the far bank, and then turn left away from the river soon returning to the car park.

2. Soon you will find a blue way-marked trail called the Craig Garth-bwlch Trail on your left. Walk gently uphill on a minor road and soon leave the woods. Follow the blue waymarked post and ignore the trail on the right. At the top of the hill and on a sharp right-hand bend there are excellent and probably one of the best views of the dam and the lake.

3. Continue along the road which carries on gently uphill for quite some time, and then starts to drop through the woods. There are some excellent views over the valley to your left (facing south). When the trail comes to a fork, ignore the left country lane to Garth Bwlch Farm but continue on the right trail following the bridlepath sign.

4. The track descends to rejoin the original blue way-

marked track at a T junction, where you turn right. When you reach a road and turn right; after about 200 metres, look out for way-marked paths (Glyndŵr's Way and Pererindod Melangell Walk) back through the forest on your right, and follow them. The trail goes through the forest and becomes steep and strenuous. Going through the forest there are a couple of options, but they lead to the same place.

5. After about a kilometre, you come to a five-way junction at the edge of the forest. You take the minor way marked path down hill (north-east) and get a fantastic view of the dam and lake. The trail leads back to Llanwddyn village and towards the car park, which is less than a kilometre away.

Originally published in
Walks in and around the Berwyn Mountains

by John Tranter

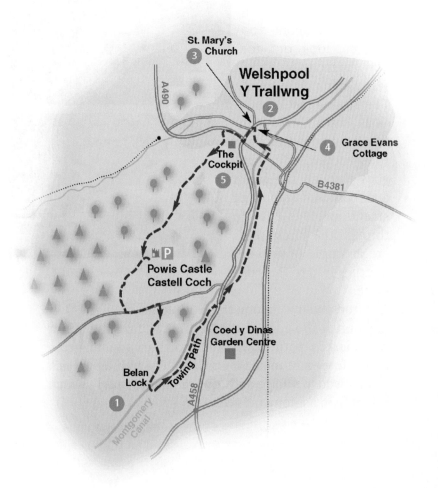

Walk 17
Powis Castle – the seat of princes

Walk details

Approx distance: *4 miles/6.6 kilometres*

Approx time: *2½ – 3 hours*

O.S. Maps: *1:50 000 Landranger Sheet 126*
1:25 000 Explorer OL 216

Start: *Powis Castle car park. Grid Ref. SJ 215 063.*

Access: *CAR: On the A483 from Newtown, take the first exit of the roundabout at the southern end of Welshpool then follow signs to Powis Castle. Take the third exit at the roundabout when travelling southwards on the Welshpool bypass. On the A458 from Llanfair Caereinion, follow signs to the town centre crossroad. Cross the road to join the A490 then follow signs for Powis Castle.*
TRAIN: From Welshpool train station, walk towards the town centre and continue walking up the street to a signpost for Powis Castle opposite Welshpool Jewellers and Rikki Lloyd Butchers. Walk through the park and you will eventually arrive at the car park.

Parking: *Powis Castle car park is free of charge. The gates to the National Trust property open at 8am and close at 7pm. Toilet facilities are at the entrance of the castle. There is an entrance fee to visit the castle and gardens.*

Going: *Easy to moderate. A good balance of hill walking and walking along the canal. Part of the walk involves walking through Welshpool town centre.*

The walk
After leaving Powis Castle Park, the walk climbs a small hill before descending through woods to the Montgomery Canal. The route then follows the towpath into Welshpool before returning to the start through the Lower Park.

Start the walk at Powis Castle car park, which is accessed from a lane off the A490 south of Welshpool. Buses and trains travel to Welshpool. The route passes through the town.

Powis Castle
The first castle here was a fortress built in the 13th century by Gruffudd ap Gwenwynwyn and his son Owain. Owain took the Norman name de la Pole and his daughter Hawys de la Pole married a Norman knight, John de Cherleton. Sir Edward Herbert acquired the castle in 1587 and he made many alterations. The Herbert family garrisoned the castle for the Royalists during the Civil War, but Parliamentary forces captured it in 1644. Heiress Lady Henrietta Herbert married Edward, the son of Clive of India, in 1784 and many of Clive's possessions were brought to the castle. There is a magnificent collection of paintings, tapestries and furniture as well as the Clive Museum. The magnificent gardens are known for their terraces, clipped yews and lead statues. Powis Castle was bequeathed to the National Trust in 1952.

Points of Interest:

[1] **The Montgomery Canal** A scheme of waterways was planned in the late 18th century to link the Severn, Mersey and Dee rivers. The Montgomeryshire Canal Act was duly authorised

and the section from Welsh Frankton to Llanymynech opened in 1796. A year later the canal passed through Welshpool, but it did not reach Newtown until 1821. The many goods transported along the Montgomery Canal included limestone, coal, timber, dairy produce and grain, and the canal at Welshpool was lined with warehouses. Road and rail took over, but the waterway was in use until 1936 when it was breached near Welsh Frankton. The canal is now known for its wildlife, and much of it is a Site of Special Scientific Interest. Its aquatic vegetation is the habitat of many dragonflies and damselflies. As you walk along the towpath, you will be following a section of the long distance footpath, The Severn Way.

[2] **Welshpool** This borderlands market town was granted a charter in 1263 by Gwenwynwyn, Prince of Powys. Many historic buildings line the broad streets, and some of them are half-timbered, dating back to the 16th century.

[3] **St Mary's Church** The parish church dates from the mid 13th century, but only the lower part of the tower remains from the original church. Inside are several monuments to the Earls of Powis. There is a memorial to Bishop William Morgan who was vicar of the church 1575-1579. He translated the Bible into

Welsh in 1588, and his birthplace, Tŷ Mawr Wybrnant, near Penmachno in north Wales, is a National Trust property. Outside St Mary's Church, opposite the church door, is a stone said to be part of the abbot's throne at Strata Marcella Abbey.

[4] **Grace Evans' Cottage** Grace Evans was a maid to the Countess of Nithsdale, who was a daughter of the Earl of Powis. The Earl of Nithsdale was condemned to death and imprisoned in the Tower of London after taking part in the 1715 Jacobite Rebellion. With the help of Grace Evans, the Countess dressed her

husband in women's clothes and smuggled him out of the tower. To thank her, the Nithsdales gave Grace Evans this cottage.

[5] **The Cockpit** The only cockpit in Wales still standing on its original site is this one in Welshpool. It was in use from the early 18th century until 1849, when cockfighting was made illegal.

Walk Directions: [-] **denotes Point of Interest**

1. From the car park, walk towards the castle, and

instead of taking the drive to the castle, go ahead along the drive signed Way Out. Go through the gate by the cattle grid then proceed to the end of the drive. There is a kissing-gate a few paces to the right of the cattle grid.

2. Turn left along the lane and pass a drive to Dyserth Hall on your right. When the entrance drive to Powis Castle is on your left, bear right over a stile next

to a field gate. Go straight ahead and follow a track, passing trees on your right. After the track bends left over a bridge, go through a gate and immediately turn right to cross a stile.

3. Walk straight ahead and soon veer left to walk uphill with the hedgerow on your right. To your left are extensive views over the Severn Valley. In the top right-hand corner of the field, climb a stile and continue along the right boundary to a kissing-gate. Walk ahead, veering slightly left up the hill, and you will soon have a fence and trees on your left. Pass a waymark and continue above the wood until you reach a wider path at a fence above the woods.

4. At the corner, climb a stile on the right into the wood. The path is steep and rope assistance is available so take care as it gradually goes downhill to a stile near a gate. Follow the trail to a kissing-gate that leads to a lane. Turn left to cross a bridge over the Montgomery Canal [1] and, after a few paces, go right through a gate onto the canal towpath.

5. Turn right along the towpath and follow it to Belan Lock. You are now walking along the Severn Way (Llwybr Hafren) footpath. Go below the road bridge (No. 122) and pass the lock and a picnic area.

6. Continue beside the canal, which

eventually bends right under a road. Cross a causeway at a nature reserve and bear left. After emerging on a lane, continue beside the canal. Powysland Museum can be seen on the opposite side of the canal. Go under a road bridge and, a little further on, cross a footbridge over the canal.

7. After passing a car park, you will arrive at a road junction in the centre of Welshpool. The route goes left here, but to your right is St Mary' Parish Church [3] and, further on, below on the right side of the church, is Grace Evans' Cottage [4].

8. Continuing on the walk, you will reach a crossroads at traffic lights. Turn right along Broad Street and pass New Street (between NatWest bank and One Stop convenience store) with its Cockpit [5] on your left. Pass the Town Hall on your right and, in

another 50 metres, turn left at a signpost for Powis Castle.

9.   Go through the gate into the Lower Park. There is a pond in trees below on the left. You may also see deer in the park which have been at Powis Castle for over 300 years. Pass through another gate and continue along the drive. Ignore the left-hand fork and walk ahead to the start of your walk at the car park.

Originally published in
National Trust Walks – southern and central Wales

by Dorothy Hamilton

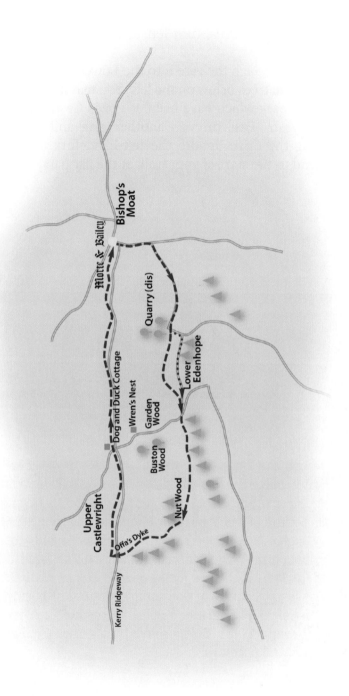

Walk 18

Kerry Ridgeway – the drovers' road

Walk details

Approx distance: *4.7 miles/7½ kilometres*

Approx time:	*2½ – 3 hour*
O.S. Maps:	1:50 000 *Landranger Sheet 137* 1:25 000 *Explorer OL 216*
Start:	*Public footpath post by metal farm gate.* *Grid Ref. SO 290 895*
Access:	*Bishop's Moat can be reached by car on the B4385 from Newtown in the west or Bishop's Castle in the east.*
Parking:	*There are no car parking facilities but parking on the side of the road will suffice.*
Going:	*Easy to moderate. A good balance between walking on quiet country lanes and through fields. Short challenging climb at Offa's Dyke.*

Before the invention of the railway, the wealth of Wales walked slowly to England. Records show that in one year in the eighteenth century 9,000 cattle swam across the Menai Strait from Anglesey and were driven to England. 6,000 left from Llŷn peninsula and 30,000 from central Wales. William Brooke, in *The True causes of our Present Distress for Provisions* (1800), estimated that in 1798 a total of 600 million pounds of beef were consumed in England. English yeomanry ate Welsh beef while Welsh farmers lived on a meagre diet of barley and potatoes.

Kerry Ridgeway Walk

The Kerry Ridgeway is one of the oldest drovers' routes across the Cambrian Mountains. The Ridgeway runs for fifteen miles, from Cider House Farm, Powys, in the west, to Bishop's Castle, Shropshire (*Swydd Amwythig*), in the east. The ridge seldom drops below 1000 feet and there are superb views of up to 70 miles depending on the weather. Our circular walk starts at Bishop's Moat, where a Motte and Bailey castle once stood guarding the track. From there you walk south and follow the strangely named River Unk through Shropshire before turning north, along a section of Offa's Dyke, climbing back to the Ridgeway and into Wales. The last part of the walk is an easy two-mile stroll along the Ridgeway, following the same route the drovers used centuries ago. Bishop's Moat is 12 miles east of Newtown (*Y Drenewydd*), 10.5 miles north of Knighton (*Trefyclo*) and 2.1 miles west of Bishop's Castle. It is possible to park on the grass verge at the road junction beside the ruined castle. It is a remote spot and there are no toilets or other facilities along the walk.

1. When you reach the crossroad, follow the sign to Bishop's Castle. In about 150 metres from the crossroad sign, park the car on a grassy lay-by near a metal gate and footpath sign on your right.

N.B. (If you want to avoid the cattle in the field, walk back to the crossroad sign and turn left with a red brick house on your left. Continue to a white house on your left).

You can leave the lane along the footpath, which crosses the field in a south-westerly direction. As you cross the field, aim for the house in the far corner. At the corner of the field, take the right-hand gate leading to a lane, and continue south-west along the lane so that you pass the house on your left.

The lane takes you downhill for 300 metres into a pretty valley. It then bears right as you follow the lane along the valley.

2.   After a further 660 metres you reach a sharp left-hand turn and a pair of white houses on the corner. There are two options; either leave the lane here and follow the footpath sign straight ahead so that the houses are on your right or carry on along the lane which avoids going through farmland, then turn right to a junction (point 4). If you follow the footpath sign, go through the metal gate on the left into a field and continue walking west so that the river is on your left. This is the River Unk, a tributary of the River Clun.

3.   Walk for 300 metres through the field and keep to the right side of the telegraph poles to a stile leading into a small conifer wood and a second stile leading to the next field. Continue following the river to a track and a shallow ford. Cross the river and go through the metal gate into the farmyard, continuing straight ahead up the yard. At the top of the yard turn right, walking west along the lane, through a metal gate and past a house on your right.

4.   After 230 metres along the lane, you reach a junction, where you leave the lane following the footpath sign pointing through a metal gate into a field that is straight ahead. The footpath forks here and you take the right-hand path along the valley.

5.   Continue for 200 metres to a gate leading to the next field, where you continue straight on, keeping the river on your right. In 250 metres you will come to a short wooden post. Cross the river so that the river is on your left and bear right for 170 metres to a metal

gate. After going through the gate, continue for 150 metres until you reach a junction with a footpath marked by yellow way-markers and white acorns. This is the Offa's Dyke Path that runs south to north and is a popular walkers' route. King Offa built the dyke as a defensive barrier against the Welsh in the eighth century, and the walk, which is 177 miles long, was opened in 1971.

6.   Turn right and walk along the path on Offa's Dyke, over a footbridge crossing the River Unk and turn left following a track uphill for a short distance to a stile on your right. Cross the stile and follow the Offa's Dyke sign pointing uphill through the wood. When you come to a crossroads in the paths, continue straight on, ignoring the blue way-markers. At the top of the challenging climb, the path emerges from the wood and you cross a kissing gate into a field. Walk along the left-hand side of the field to the next wooden gate, where the path continues between a fence on your right and the earth remains of the original dyke on your left. There are a number of large burrows in the dyke, suggesting that badgers have taken up residence.

7.   Keep walking along the path until you reach two wooden gates leading to a tarmac lane. The second gate is the border and you have just passed from Shropshire into Powys. You are now standing on the Kerry Ridgeway, which dissects the Offa's Dyke Path. Turn right along the Ridgeway so that you are walking east, in the same direction that the drovers would herd

their animals. Kerry Ridgeway was last used for droving about 150 years ago, after which railways made the practice of walking animals to England uneconomic.

Typically, drovers' routes were about 14 feet wide, so the stock had room to move and the animals could find some grazing. Although the Kerry Ridgeway is now a metalled single-track lane, there is very little traffic and the original size of the track is clearly visible.

8.   Continue walking east along the Ridgeway and look north where you will see a strange group of four hills. These are the hills of Churchstoke (Yr Ystog). According to a passing walker they are also known as the 'Devil's Chair', because according to folklore the Devil always sits there to rest when the hills are hidden by cloud.

9.   Further on the lane descends and you pass 'Dog and Duck Cottage' on your left. The Ridgeway then climbs again, and after a further 2.1 km you arrive back at the starting point of the walk. At the crossroad, the castle mound is on your left next to the farm. It is the small mound covered by shrubbery and trees. The castle was built around 1120 by the Bishop of Hereford and originally had a bailey that was 100 metres by 65 metres, demonstrating the importance of the Kerry Ridgeway in ancient times. It is believed that the Kerry Ridgeway is older than the Dark Age and Iron Age earthworks that lie nearby, and there are Bronze Age burials and a stone circle near the ridge.

Originally published in
Walking with Welsh Legends – Central Wales

by Graham Watkins

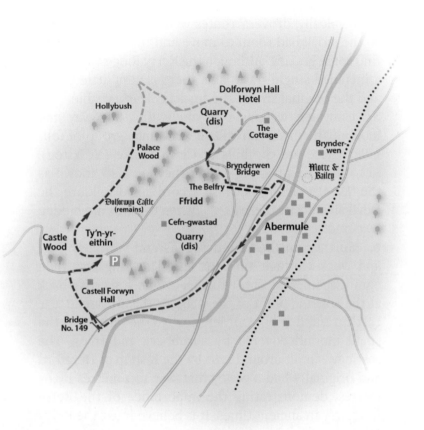

Walk 19
Dolforwyn Castle – Llywelyn's dream

Walk details

Approx distance: *3 miles/4.8 kilometres*

Approx time: *2 – 2½ hours*

O.S. Maps: *1:50 000 Landranger Sheet 136*
1:25 000 Explorer OL 215

Start: *Castell Dolforwyn car park.*
Grid Ref. SO 154 949

Access: *Accessed from the A483. One mile west of Abermiwl*
and 34 miles north east of Newtown. There is a
train station in Newtown.

Parking: *Car park area for a maximum of four or five cars*
opposite the footpath to the castle. Free car park.

Going: *Moderate. Fairly challenging walk up to the castle*
remains. Hillside walks but does get easier along the
flat footpath by the canal.

Dolforwyn Castle Walk

This is a pleasant country walk that begins by climbing a short distance to Dolforwyn castle and then takes you through woodland before descending to the Montgomery Canal and the Afon Hafren. Dolforwyn castle is located near the A483 four miles north-east of Newtown and ten miles south-west of Welshpool, and not far from Montgomery (*Trefaldwyn*). Follow the CADW signpost for the castle near the village of Abermule (*Abermiwl*) and drive along the lane for two-thirds of a mile to a small car park where the walk begins. You join the river at a bridge that proudly boasts it is the 'Second Iron Bridge', built in 1852. The walk then continues along the canal towpath, between the river and the canal, and finally, after a short climb, returns to the car park below the castle. Parking is free but there are no facilities along the route.

1. Leave your car and walk north-east along the lane for a few steps to the signposted track on the left. Follow the track uphill through a gate. After 100 metres the track turns left and you walk south-west for 180 metres past a house on your right and arrive at a wooden gate. Go through the gate and follow the path straight on for another 200 metres, where you turn right along a grassy track leading up to the castle. This track was once the main street of the town that sat below the castle and was lined with timber-framed, thatched buildings.

The castle was built towards the end of the thirteenth century by Llywelyn ap Gruffudd, Prince of Gwynedd. Llywelyn was declared the 'Prince of Wales' by a convention of Welsh leaders in 1258, and was so recognised by Henry III in the Treaty of Montgomery (1267). His ambition was to build his capital here in Dolforwyn, above the central valley of his county. It was also a border fortress designed as a stronghold against the English. As you explore the ruin it becomes apparent that the castle was not built for comfort but a bastion that would be difficult to overcome. The English king, Edward I, besieged Dolforwyn castle in 1277 and captured it. Ownership of the castle and town then passed to Roger Mortimer. The town was abandoned in 1279 when Roger Mortimer started the construction of Newtown further down the valley.

Once you have explored the castle, continue

north-east along the track on the north side of the ruin. As you reach the end of the castle wall, a footpath, which you take, continues straight on through the trees for 60 metres to a stile. Take care as the path is overgrown and hardly visible. Go through the gate and follow the path downhill across a field, passing gorse bushes on your right and continuing north-east for 200 metres until you reach a large oak tree in the middle of the field. As you pass the oak tree turn north and walk downhill beside a fence to the bottom of the field and a footbridge over a stream.

2.   On the other side of the stream, continue straight on uphill to a metal gate leading to a lane. Turn right along the lane for 10 m and then turn right through a wooden gate leading to a footpath signposted to Abermiwl, where you walk east, downhill, through a field to a pond at the bottom of the field. Walk through the gate and across the pond dam so that the pond is on your right. On the far side of the dam you pass through two more gates leading into a wood. Continue along the footpath as it follows the edge of the wood and takes you east into the next valley.

3.   The footpath continues for 250 metres to a gate where it turns to the south and after 60 metres you go through another gate leading to a driveway. Walk down the drive to the lane where you turn right and then immediately left along a lane with a 'dead end' sign.

Alternative Route: The trail can be overgrown and impassable therefore an alternative route may be needed. This trail is completely on country lanes rather than through fields like the other route. From the gate and Castell Dolforwyn signpost leading to a country lane (Grid Ref. SO 153 954), keep walking

 northwards to a junction with the sign 'Hollybush Penswyddfa'. Turn right and walk for 700 metres until you reach a junction with a CADW sign (green Celtic cross symbol). Turn right and continue for 300 metres to a lane on your left (Grid Ref. SO 157 952).

4.   Continue along the lane for 200 metres until you reach 'The Belfry', an unusual house on your right. Leave the lane through the gate along with the 'Abermiwl & Dolforwyn Castle' signpost on your left opposite the house. Walk 120 metres down the left-hand side of the next field, aiming for a gate in the bottom left hand corner.

5.   At the bottom of the field, go through the gate, cross the busy main road carefully and through the gate on the far side of the road, leading into a small field. Turn left and walk 60 metres across the field towards a hedge and gate. Go through the gate onto a road and turn right for a few steps. Cross the first bridge, over the canal, and turn right walking down the slope to join the canal towpath.

6.   You are now walking on part of the Severn Way, a 210-mile long-distance walk along the river. As you join the towpath, look at the cast-iron bridge over the river on your left. It bears the words:

'This second iron bridge constructed in the County of Montgomery was erected in the year 1852'

Abraham Derby III built the first, more famous, Ironbridge across the Severn at Ironbridge Gorge in 1779.

The canal was constructed to transport lime to the upper Severn Valley to improve its agricultural yield. Eventually the canal extended from Newtown to Franklin Junction on the Llangollen Canal, a distance of 33 miles. The canal was profitable until the 1914–18 war, when it started to lose money. It was abandoned in 1936 when a major leak occurred at Franklin Bridge. The canal is of historical significance and considerable restoration has been undertaken during the last fifty years.

7.   Follow the canal towpath for 500 metres until the canal turns right and passes under the road, while the footpath goes straight on. Continue along the footpath for another 100 metres where the path turns right and passes under the flyover, and rejoin the canal on the far side. Walk a further 550 metres along the towpath until you reach bridge number 149, just before the second set of lock gates. Go over the bridge, through the gate, and turn left along the lane for a few steps before turning right, through a gate into the wood, following the footpath sign to Castell Dolforwyn.

8.   The footpath now goes north east for 450 metres and climbs through a field towards a gate at the top. Keep to the right side of the field following the hedgerow. There are some fantastic views of the Severn Valley from this point. Go through the gate and turn right along the lane for 700 metres until you arrive back at the car park and the starting point of your walk.

Originally published in
Walking with Welsh Legends – Central Wales

by Graham Watkins

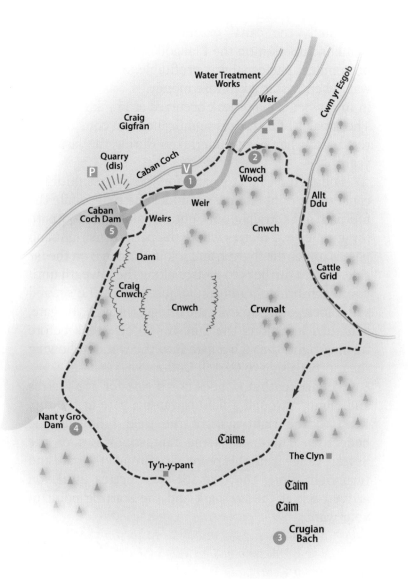

Walk 20

Elan Valley Visitor Centre – a short valley walk

Walk details

Approx distance: *3½ miles/5½ kilometres*

Approx time:	*2½ hours*
O.S. Maps:	*1:50 000 Landranger 147* *1:25 000 Explorer OL 200*
Start:	*Elan Valley Visitor Centre* *Grid Ref. SN 928 646*
Access:	*From Rhayader town centre, follow the B4518 (signed for the Elan Valley) to the Visitor Centre, which is signposted on the left hand side.*
Parking:	*Car park at the Visitor Centre (£1 fee).*
Going:	*Easy to moderate – involves about 200m of ascent (rising to about 250m if you opt for the diversion into Cnwch Wood Nature Trail). Although quite short, this walk affords numerous opportunities to take detours to gain a real flavour of the nature of the Elan Valley. Walking boots strongly recommended – there are some sections that may be slippery when wet.*

A fairly short walk, concentrating on the dams of the Elan Valley, with a twist in the tail of the history of the dams. It is also possible to combine this walk with a visit to the Elan Valley Visitor Centre and the Cnwch Wood Nature Trail.

Points of Interest:

[1] **Elan Valley Visitor Centre** The Elan Valley Visitor Centre contains a café, public conveniences, gift shop, and various exhibits detailing the local wildlife and the complexities of the Elan Valley water management scheme. It is possible to obtain fishing permits here for the reservoirs in the valley, which are stocked with brown trout. For the walker, packed lunches can be obtained from the café, and books and leaflets can be bought from the shop and information desk detailing many walks in the area of the Centre. Most are very short, of about a mile or so, but the Elan Valley Trail stretches for five miles (eight kilometres) from the Visitor Centre to Penygarreg Dam. An extension to the Visitor's Centre was opened in May 1997 by the botanist David Bellamy.

[2] **Cnwch Wood Nature Trail** This delightful trail follows a well-managed path through the southern half of Cnwch Wood, which was designated a Site of Special Scientific Interest in 1965. Consisting mostly of various species of oak, the trail is rich in woodland fauna and flora, though is perhaps most interesting for the rich variety of bird life deliberately attracted to the area by the use of nesting boxes. It may be possible here to see redstarts, flycatchers, nuthatches and owls. Much natural history information is provided for the walker via the use of information panels along the route, of which there are no less than ten. Although a diversion along this trail would add a little distance to the walk, it is strongly recommended.

[3] **Crugian Bach** At about 450m above sea level, Crugian Bach does not present us with a particularly

spectacular high point or summit, but it does provide some great views in all directions, and if it is rather breezy (which is not unusual around here!) it should be possible to find a place among the crags to eat your sandwiches with a certain degree of shelter. The area of Crugian Bach contains many hillocks, and it is necessary to nip from hillock to hillock to gain the best vantage point for each direction. This is one of those places whose mood is dictated by the weather. On a clear, sunny day it is positively cheerful here, but on a dull day the area radiates a bleakness that is almost malevolent. When dark clouds threaten, Allt Goch to the east broods menacingly, while the cairn on Cnwch to the north west almost appears a harbinger of doom. Yet, when the clouds disperse and the sun shines, the whole area lights up to provide the perfect picnic spot.

About six or so miles away to the south west, clear weather would allow you to see the twin cairns of Drygarn Fawr, which at 645m above sea level is the highest point in the area.

[4] **Nant y Gro Dam** A small coffer dam designed originally to provide a water supply and hydroelectric power to the Elan Village (which itself was built to house the workers on the Elan Valley water scheme at the end of the Victorian era), the Nant y Gro Dam is no more, and its ruins remind us of perhaps one of the strangest episodes in the history of the Elan Valley. The peaceful surroundings of hills, woodland and expanses of water that make up the valley may seem an unlikely place to

become a top secret centre for the development of experimental forms of warfare, but in 1943 that was exactly what happened, and the valley was to play an important part in the planning of one of the most well-known episodes of World War II. It so happened that Nant y Gro Dam was of a similar design to the dams of the Ruhr Valley in Germany, which were the target of the famous Dambuster raid, and it was here that Barnes Wallis collected vital information for the development of the unique bouncing bomb that was used to such dramatic effect in that raid. The dam, of course, did not survive the experiments, and today only its ruins remain. Across the Caban Coch Reservoir, you may be able to see the Foel Tower, a deceptively complicated device that ensures that the water supply from the Elan Valley to Birmingham can be transported solely by the force of gravity by providing a sufficiently elevated outlet to the filter beds. Across the reservoir at this point you can also see what appears to be a road bridge. However, under the bridge is the submerged Garreg Ddu Dam, the top of which is usually about 12m below the waterline. This dam also plays a vital part in ensuring that the Foel Tower outlet is provided with water at all times. Better views of these structures can be had from the descent down from Crugian Bach.

[5] **Caban Coch Dam** The dam is 186m long, 38m thick at its base, and rises some 37m above the river bed, allowing the reservoir a capacity of about eight thousand million gallons over an area of 500 acres. It was built as part of the Elan Valley scheme of reservoirs at the end of the Victorian era, and opened on July 21st 1904 by King Edward VII.

Walk Directions:

[-] **denotes Point of Interest**

1. From the car park at the Visitor Centre [1], walk back north-east in the direction of the road to the Bailey Bridge that crosses Afon Elan. Cross

the bridge and proceed to the wooden gate, then our main route heads off immediately to the left onto a waymarked footpath through the north end of Cnwch Wood. (There is a possible diversion here, however, which would allow you to visit the Cnwch Wood Nature Trail [2] adding about 1.5 mls or 2.5 km to your walk; to do so, take the more obvious path south west, then follow the obvious zig-zag path uphill through the wood to the end of the trail, before retracing your steps back to our main route.) To continue along our main route, turn left at the gate and follow the footpath over a stile, tending uphill along a wire fence. Arriving at a junction of paths, keep left (follow the red arrow sign) and proceed to a stream. There are stepping-stones here but they can be slippery. The path continues uphill fairly obviously to a grassy track near the road. Turn right onto this grassy track (following a line of telegraph poles) and continue uphill to the country lane at Grid Ref. SN 934 646.

2. Turn right onto the lane, and follow this south, then south-east for nearly 1 km (just over half a mile) over a cattle grid to a junction with a smaller lane on the right (at Grid Ref. SN 937 639). Approach a bridlepath sign and an arrow inscribed "Clyn", turn

right here, then after about 75m bear right again, through a metal gate, to head uphill roughly west. Continue south-west, along a narrow metalled road to a gate at the edge of woodland (at Grid Ref. SN 931 633). Pass through the gate and onto Comin Llanwrthwl which is open moorland protected by the National Trust. The common is part of the Abergwesyn Commons which are rich in archaeology, from Bronze Age ritual sites to deserted medieval villages. Wherever you walk you're likely to come across a cairn, a stone circle or standing stone and other evidence of human activity dating back hundreds, if not thousands, of years.

3. Continue forward for about 25m to a junction of tracks. To the left a footpath heads off south-east along

the edge of the forestry and to the right the main bridleway heads off roughly south-west towards Ty'n-y-Pant, but there is also a smaller path leading off south almost straight ahead. Take this smaller track south towards the crags of Crugian Bach (Grid Ref. SN 931 628), passing two rather inconspicuous cairns (presumably of Bronze Age origin) on the left. The crags and hillocks of Crugian Bach [3] do not represent the highest point in the area, but they afford a fine view in all directions.

4.   From Crugian Bach, you need to rejoin the main track leading towards Ty'n-y-pant. The easiest way to do this is to retrace your steps to the gate at Grid Ref. SN 931 633. However, the going is not too difficult here and you can save a little distance by striking off between north and north-west to rejoin the obvious main track somewhere to the east of the ruined farmhouse of Ty'n-y-pant. In clear weather the best routes will be obvious, and you can use sheeptracks to make the going over the heather and tussocks easier. In mist, care should be taken here – you should tend more north than north-west and take it easy to avoid turning an ankle or tripping over. Either way, you want to arrive at the junction of paths at Grid Ref. SN 929 632, where a bridleway is signposted left towards the south-west and a footpath is signposted to the right almost due west. Take the footpath west, passing immediately north of Ty'n-y-pant, then continue to head towards the woodlands in front of you, tending very steeply down north-east to follow the line of the forestry down to Caban-coch Reservoir at Grid Ref. SN 922 636. Here is the ruin of Nant y Glo Dam [4].

5.   Follow the waymarked path along the bank of Caban-coch Reservoir east of north towards Caban-coch Dam [5]. Just beyond the old stone viewing platform at the top of the dam, a stile on the left leads to a path descending steeply down to a footbridge across the Elan. Initially here there are some crumbling stone steps requiring care, and then newer wooden steps make the going easier. Cross the footbridge, pass round the building and head back north of east back to the start point at the Visitor Centre.

Facilities:
The Elan Valley, and the town of Rhayader itself, are well supplied with places to stay and to eat and drink. The Tourist Information Centre in Rhayader should be able to supply up-to-date information regarding the availability of local accommodation. The Elan Valley Visitor Centre also contains many facilities (see above).

Safety Notes:
Virtually the entire walk follows well-defined paths, and therefore there should be no problem with navigation even in the worst weather. About the only place that mist could cause problems would be around Crugian Bach. If you lose you bearings here, simply head slightly west of north. Eventually you must hit the main bridlepath leading to Ty'n-y-pant. Alternatively, you could head due west, in which case sooner or later you must hit either Caban-coch Reservoir, or (more likely) the forestry on its eastern bank. Then simply follow the line of forestry slightly north to the path along the bank of the reservoir. If you head west, though, great care must be taken over the moorland – there are many tussocks and rocks to trip the unwary, and some sections are very steep.

Originally published in
Circular Walks in Central Wales

by Stephen Edwards